Table of Contents.

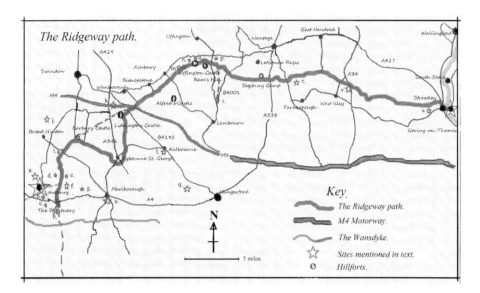

Map showing The Ridgeway path and places mentioned in the text.

a. Windmill Hill.
b. Silbury Hill.
c. West Kennett Long Barrow.
d. Monkton Down crop marks.
e. Overton Down experimental earthwork.
f. Fyfield Down sharpening stone.
g. Devil's Den tomb.
h. The Sanctuary temple.
i. Broad Hinton white horse hill figure.
j. Binknoll Castle.
k. Badbury Wick Roman villa site.
l. Aldbourne village pond. 'The Moonraker's Tale'.
m. Wayland's Smithy tomb.
n. Dragon Hill & The Manger, Uffington.
o. The White Horse of Uffington.
p. Blowing Stone, Kingston Lisle.
q. Littlecote Roman villa & Elizabethan manor house, Chilton Foliat.
r. Lord Wantage's monument.
s. 'The Frenchman's Tale'.
t. Lambourne 'Seven Barrows'.
u. Marlborough Castle mound.
v. Wild camping site & police incident.

Tales of the Ridgeway.

Introduction.

First let me set the scene. This compilation of stories, anecdotes and snippets of information are based on personal experiences, observations and knowledge gained over more than fifty years. The Ridgeway in question is that which runs between Streatley-on-Thames in Berkshire to Avebury in Wiltshire and forms the south-western section, stretching some forty miles, of the Icknield Way the pre-historic track that originates up in Norfolk around The Wash. The eastern half of the route runs across what is known as The Berkshire Downs, although much of it now lies within Oxfordshire, the result of the county boundary changes imposed back in the early 1970's, more of this later.

I was born in Swindon in 1954, the youngest of five children. My father was a worker in the Great Western Railway workshops my mother, a traditional housewife of the period. Brought up and living in Swindon through into the early 70's my horizons were quite literally dominated by the Downs. To the uninitiated, these are the chalk hills to the south and east of Swindon that forms the north-facing escarpment along the top of which The Ridgeway runs. Prominent on this skyline some six miles distant and at 277m, 910ft in old money, the highest point along the whole stretch of The Ridgeway covered by this article is the Iron Age period hill-fort that crowns Liddington Hill. But just as if to make absolutely sure your identification is correct, the clump of trees that stand alongside the earthworks confirm it. To an urban child surrounded by smoke, terraced houses and people, lots of people, the Downs offered an escape from the drabness and noise. It was this view of green hills and large blue skies over the Downs that helped fire my imagination, leading me into a life of walking, archaeology and exploration of wild places.

Swindon in the late 50's was rapidly changing from being the major Victorian railway engineering centre developed by Isambard Kingdom Brunel. Up until then Swindon had grown gradually, with additional light industry and electronics businesses being a spin-off from war production. With its prime location on the Great Western Railway it was well placed to become a centre for the offices, warehousing and distribution centres of many large London based businesses of the day. W. H. Smith, Vickers, Brown Brothers, Garrards and Plessey were just a few, but following the construction of the M4 motorway, in the late 60's and early 70's major world players have moved in adding to the economic success of the town.

Back in the early 60's I well remember the hooter that was sounded in order to call the men back to work in 'the factory' at dinner time. 'The factory' was the name given to the railway workshops by the workforce. Dinnertime was midday, lunch being a word virtually unknown and unused by the working classes at that time. The hooter was sounded with a five-minute interval and could be heard anything up to three to four miles away if the wind was right! Stand in the street at the beginning of dinnertime near to 'the factory' gates and you were likely as not to be run over by one of the hundreds of men on bicycles racing to get home for dinner! The most chilling memory for me was of the high red brick walls that surrounded the workshops making them look like a prison. To many who worked inside those walls that was exactly what 'the factory' was, especially once the gates were closed behind them. Those same walls now enclose parts of the retail village that has been developed on the site of the former railway works and sidings. In Rodbourne, where 'the factory' was located either side of the road and the railway line from London, Paddington to the West Country ran overhead, the diesel fumes from double-decker buses mixed with those from the growing volume of cars made breathing nigh on impossible, especially if you were like me 'knee high to a grasshopper' as my dad used to say. This then was the atmosphere and environment I was brought up in. Is it then any wonder that I longed to see what was over the horizon, to breathe fresh air and experience the sound of silence?

The author in 1978 (courtesy of The Hastings Observer).

1. Early days exploring The Ridgeway.

My first experience of The Ridgeway was being taken up onto the Downs by my parents. These early trips were accomplished using local buses to get us as near to the foot of the Downs, occasionally catching the Marlborough or Hungerford services which crossed The Ridgeway at Chiseldon and Liddington. Our days out were therefore governed by the rural bus services, the rail line to Marlborough having been closed down many years previously. By this means we accessed points along The Ridgeway near to Liddington on the A419, the B4192 as it is now, and at various places along the A345, now the A346. This was the Roman road running south from Cirencester (Corinivm) through to Mildenhall (Cvnetio) near Marlborough, at which point it divided, the southern route continuing on via Salisbury (Sorviodvnvm) to Poole Harbour in Dorset, the south eastern route going by way of Winchester (Venta) and subdividing yet again to give access to the important Roman sea ports of Bittern in Southampton (Glavsentvm) and Chichester (Noviomagvs). The Devizes bus ran parallel to The Ridgeway for most of its course from Wroughton to Avebury along the A361, now the A4361. This then was the furthest one could hope to cover in a day, The Ridgeway towards Streatley being beyond reach unless private transport was available, or several days.

These early forays were usually family affairs that included my parents and occasionally an older brother. On these excursions we would cover several miles on foot exploring the local churches and sites of archaeological and historical interest, stopping at public houses for refreshment if the opportunity presented itself. At no time do I remember seeing my parents use a map, following public footpath signs along with one's nose appeared to suffice! Mind you, it's fair to say we were following in the footsteps of my mother's family who had lived and worked on the land hereabouts for the previous three centuries and more. Even so, I remember more than once us being lost in the network of fields and woods that made up the approaches to the Downs just south of Swindon.

One particular occasion stands out when we had my mother's father with us. He would have been retired at the time, previously a boilermaker in the Great Western. We had attempted to find our way from Coate Water (constructed in 1822 to serve the local canal system), via Hodson to Chiseldon along the line of the old railway. Coate Water in those days presented a swampy backwater at its southern end, occasionally frequented by hardened anglers in wellies. Hodson was normally approached by means of the lane that skirted Coate, but my parents were not to be deterred. We walked round the east side of the reservoir after first paying the few pennies entrance charge made by Swindon Corporation, and then somehow fought our way through eventually emerging out onto the lane. The day being sunny and hot we soon dried out as we crossed the lane and continued along the line of the defunct railway. Rampant undergrowth and heat was to be the main factors in slowing our progress, those and granddad's age. At one point we left the railway and tramped through a cornfield. The corn being higher than me, my parents were highly amused when I took to jumping up and down in order to see the way ahead. We regained the railway just before it entered a cutting. Once back on the railway track progress was good, until that is we arrived in Chiseldon. Here we had to scramble up the steep wall of another cutting in order to access the village and the other end of the lane from Hodson. My parents struggled up the bank as it was, but you should have seen my granddad. He made quite a sight huffing and puffing up that bank, his face turning purple and the sweat pouring off him ... pushed by dad and pulled by mum.... dressed in his Sunday best, a brown serge pin striped three piece suit! Needless to say, at this point in the proceedings he had removed his jacket and tie and rolled up his shirtsleeves. Quite apart from the obvious fear of him having a coronary, he looked as if any second he would overbalance and topple back down the bank. However, the top was safely reached. It was then decided to call it a day and make our way back to Coate along the lane.

At Hodson we sought refreshment in the Calley Arms, which was something of a strange experience. If my memory serves me correctly the public house was undergoing a complete rebuild. The old building was set back off the lane with a couple of steps up to the front door and was continuing to serve the public as a new extension was being built directly in front, effectively encapsulating it. Scaffolding along with noise and dust was everywhere, the space between the two buildings being no more than a narrow gap. Those were the days when planning laws hadn't foreseen the demise of so many old vernacular buildings; when progress meant sweeping away the old and bringing in the new, with little thought for our heritage. As was the custom, I sat outside with my ginger beer and crisps come rain or shine. Luckily for me the day was hot and sunny. In those days few rural public houses allowed children to cross the threshold as they rarely had a 'family room', many didn't even have inside toilets!

Many such sorties followed some utilising bicycles. During that period, the 60's, we seldom used, or owned, any specific equipment designed for walking or cycling other than a cycling cape made of plastic. Ordinary shoes, sandals or plimsolls, the equivalent of trainers today, were worn for the most part. I experienced blisters on more than one occasion due mainly to cheap thin nylon socks. Quilted nylon anoraks, duffle coats and the like were worn, but none of these of course were waterproof. My mother would carry a clear plastic mac or hat. Any spare clothing and sandwiches, drinks etcetera, would be carried in a duffle bag or ordinary shopping bag. Only towards the end of the sixties did I acquire my first leather walking boots and a proper anorak. The former were really oil resistant work boots made by a firm called Tuff, the latter was a pull-on cotton affair with gusset strap, draw-cord waist and a hood, made by Fellstaff, or was it Bellstaff? Kirk Douglas had worn an identical anorak in the film The Heroes of Telemark, which impressed me! Both were got prior to attending a week's outward-bound course with my school in the Brecon Beacons. I attended these courses two years running during which time I acquired better map reading and compass skills, plus a greater thirst for adventure. It was at this time I became involved in orienteering, once competing on behalf of my school in a national competition held in the Forest of Dean. On that occasion my team mate and me misread the very first instruction and became hopelessly disorientated, only finding our way back to the finishing point and our coach just minutes prior to its departure time!

It wasn't until I left school at the age of fifteen, in 1969, and started work that I was able to acquire specialised clothing and equipment, mainly obtained from the ex-army and navy stores. One of the first items acquired was a simple canvas unframed rucksack. I couldn't't wait to try it out so promptly filled it with dirty washing and two house bricks for added weight and went on a twelve mile walk up onto The Ridgeway above Wroughton. The unpadded straps didn't half cut into my shoulders! Due to restricted funds and the high costs of the real thing, my first tent was purchased jointly with a friend from Milletts. This was made of orange coloured cotton and sold as a 'child's play tent'. It was just under six-foot long by three foot wide by three foot high with wooden poles but no ridgepole, sewn-in ground sheet or flysheet. That tent went on to serve me for the next five years or so. Eventually it was put to its designed use by my children, by which time it was terribly faded and sported patches in an attempt to cover holes where it had been gnawed by mice during storage.

As mentioned above, bicycles were used to cover more ground or to reach points not served by buses. During one such outing on a beautiful summer's day I had the use of a borrowed bicycle that was to prove too small for me; the result of which was that I frequently hit my knees on the handlebars. My parents were using ordinary sit-up and beg models with three speeds. We had set out via Wanborough to follow the back lanes linking the tiny hamlets and villages strung out along the spring-line beneath the escarpment, basically the route of the Icknield Way. Our destination was Whitehorse Hill above Uffington. We passed through Little Hinton and Bishopstone, where we stopped to admire the ducks on the village pond. Then it was on to Ashbury where a further stop was made for refreshments at the village inn. Although these settlements in the early 60's were being lived in by people working in good jobs in Swindon, they remained by and large primarily farming communities and a little scruffy. By the end of the 60's however the rapid development of Swindon, coupled with the opening of the M4, had made a huge impact on these previously quiet rural communities. The change in lifestyles and the resulting gentrification has led to property prices rising at an alarming rate, with commuting into Swindon and London becoming the norm. What would be a simple brick and stone-built cottars dwelling or estate cottage then, now would command an arm and a leg to buy! It's the same story to be seen throughout much of the United Kingdom that is served by fast road connections to the cities.

Our ride so far had taken the best part of the morning, due in part to my mother having to walk up most of the steep short hilly bits *and* down the other side. She put this down to inefficient gears and brakes when in reality she was never really happy on a bike at the best of times, her lack of balance causing her to wobble alarmingly. Anyway she persevered and we at last reached The Manger, the steep sided coomb cutting into the foot of Whitehorse Hill. From here we glimpsed the shape of the chalk hill figure carved into the side of the hill, distorted by our angle of view. The walk to the top was slow, but once there worth every effort. Spectacular views were had across the Vale of White Horse to the north, west and east, with the Thames basin laid out below us and the Cotswolds and Chiltern Hills far off on the horizon. Over all was a huge blue sky with white billowing cumulus clouds building to the north, forming a backdrop to an awe inspiring scene. This for me was one of the few occasions when I had been in such a lofty location. From our vantage point the patchwork of fields below us in the vale appeared to me like a scene from out of a war film; you know the sort of thing, ace fighter pilot in his Spitfire coming into land with part of one wing blown away and flames coming from the engine cowling!

Such were the daydreams of a ten year old back in the mid 60's. It was only once I had recovered my senses that I was able to take in my immediate surroundings.

Below us was the tremendous sinuous figure of the horse. The green turf cut away and the chalk exposed to form the outlines of the beast from close up left a lot to the imagination. The overall design was difficult to make out and things were not made any better by the rudimentary wire fence surrounding it. It was some time before I was convinced that we were standing just above its head, the beaklike mouth to our left, the large circular depression gleaming white directly beneath us, its eye. That was the point at which I was told by my parents in their simple straightforward matter of fact way the story relating to the cutting of the horse, and the folklore attached to making a wish upon its eye. I don't remember the exact words they used, but no doubt they would have gone along the lines "He's some beast, isn't he? They say he was cut on the orders of King Alfred to celebrate his victory over the Danes". That would have been about all that was said on the origins and history of the horse apart from mentioning that the villagers of Uffington scoured it, traditionally every seven years. Quite who "they" were I was at a loss to know. If I wanted any greater detail or other 'facts', that was left up to me to find out about over the following years. As for the folklore attached to wishing on the horse's eye my parents were just as succinct, but on this point I was quite prepared to believe them. Stepping over the wire we approached the eye and stood round it. "Now Clive, you stand on his eye and close yours. Now you make a wish, anything you want, but don't tell anyone or us. Repeat the wish three times to yourself and if you don't tell anyone your wish will come true". Well, believe that and you'll believe anything. But being a gullible kid what would you expect? The long and the short of it was that I stood there and made my wish. "Now remember, you keep your wish a secret and you'll get whatever it was you wished for", my mother's words or something very much like that. How long I would have to wait for the wish to come true I had no idea, but there's blind faith for you. As it happens my wish did come true some two years later when I was presented with my very own bicycle as a birthday present. It was second-hand, twelve quid off a neighbour. The gears didn't operate as they should which meant only three worked fulfilling my wish to the letter, a bicycle with a three speed!

More will be said in greater detail of White Horse Hill and The Manger later, suffice it to say that on this occasion we made our way back down via the access road holding our bikes back in order to keep together with mother who was walking! Our return journey took us via Kingston Lisle and the foot of Blowingstone Hill. Just a little up the road on the left from the crossroads is Blowingstone Cottage, in the front garden of which stands a large knobbly sarcen stone containing holes. One of these holes goes right through the stone following a tortuous route and if a person is of sound body, they can purse their lips to it and by blowing as if it were a trumpet, produce a tremendous bellowing noise that can be heard for miles around. Well that's the type of purple prose you'll read in any of the various guidebooks and literature that was current at the time of our visit. Local legend says the stone was dragged down from off the Downs where it had been used by King Alfred to summon his troops prior to battle, no doubt the battle culminating in his victory over the Danes. That is as may be, in reality the stone is a large block of natural sandstone local to the area. As to the noise one can obtain from it, you really do have to be able to play a trumpet or similar to stand any chance of getting a good result, but it is possible. Sarcen by the way is believed to be a corruption of Saracen. The name is mediaeval in origin and is thought by some people to have been applied to the many isolated stones found on and around The Ridgeway because they appear as if by magic, no sandstone outcrop or strata being present in situ; Saracens being looked upon as mystical people by the returning Crusaders of the middle ages, magicians if you like. Another local name for these stones is 'Grey Wethers', in other words grey sheep, as from a distance that's exactly what they look like. We returned via Uffington, Watchfield and Shrivenham, and finally Stratton St. Margaret, a round trip of some thirty miles, although my father said it was nearer forty. My bum was not quite the same for some time, not to mention my knees which were bruised from coming into contact with the handlebars. Ah those were the days!

It was thanks to such trips out with my parents as those above that I was inspired to search out and research the local history and archaeology. They gave me the initial push without even thinking about it, but it was left up to me to fill in the gaps in their knowledge, or lack of, I should say. The one thing I never lacked in my childhood was a sense of adventure and discovery, and that was due in no great part to my parents. It was my mother who was the one for ever wanting to take off into the wild blue yonder, to see what was over the next hill, what was round the next corner. My father for his part was quite content to follow, to be the backup. These very different outlooks were in no small degree due I am sure to their experiences during the war. To understand what has influenced my outlook it is important to know a little of the background environment that my parents had lived through.

My parents were both born in 1920 and had met in 1940. Dad was an only child and had enlisted in the Territorial Army just prior to the outset of the war along with a 'pal' from his home village of Whittlesey, near Peterborough. Dad and his pal served together initially in the Northamptonshire Regiment but were separated when they volunteered for the newly formed Commandos, my father passing the fitness training but failing the eyesight test. It was while convalescing following being wounded in France that my father fetched up in Swindon (my mother's home town) and as they say, the rest is history. They married in 1942. My mother was the older of two children and at the time was working on the Great Western Railway, like her father, but later went into working on aircraft assembly. In March 1944 my father was sent overseas again, this time to Naples to serve in the Italian campaign centred on Monte Casino. This was followed by a brief time in Egypt. In October 1944, when back in Europe, he was reported missing in action. Not until February 1945 was it confirmed that he had in fact been taken as a prisoner of war. My mother had waited five months not knowing whether he was dead or alive! They were finally reunited in the summer of 1945, but it was to be June 1946 before he was discharged so as they could lead a normal life together, normal that is for the times. My father like many others of his generation found it difficult to cope with mundane life after having gone through so much, my mother likewise. Both had experienced a wider world, one of opportunity and change, but both now found themselves having to revert to the stereotyped roles expected of them. My father settled for a quiet life, thankful to be alive, and looked forward to better times, my eldest brother having been born in 1946. My mother though I feel never quite adjusted to being the traditional housewife and mother. I think she resented having had no real time to get to know dad, no time in which to explore her emotions wants and aspirations. Those were hard times in many ways, much harder than anything I have had to go through, and far harder than the present generation has to deal with. It explains to me my mother's need to get out of the house and explore, to travel (albeit in a limited way) and live for the moment, and also the mental illness's both my parents suffered.

I went on to marry and have three children of my own, to lead a life somewhat different from the norm with archaeology forming a vital part, active membership of local archaeological groups and museums being a feature of wherever I lived, culminating in graduating from my BSc. Hons. Degree in Heritage Conservation when a mature student at the age of forty four. During the past thirty years or so I have paid return visits to the Downs, in particular the Ridgeway. Holidays and short breaks have been planned to incorporate walks, site seeing and the odd bit of camping. Old haunts and places that hold many fond memories for me I have shared with friends and family alike. Looking back, and that to a greater degree is what these tales are doing, my decisions in life can be seen to have been directly affected by the experiences of those of my parents. So, with the above in mind I hope that you, the reader, will go on to read the following pages and enjoy my reminiscences relating to The Ridgeway and its immediate environs.

2. Archaeology opens my eyes.

To many, The Ridgeway is just a track giving access to the Downs for leisure activities such as walking the dog, the children and themselves. Car parks at strategic points make such access evermore easy. But The Ridgeway is far more than just a green track, an un-adopted road, it was and still is a long distance route linking Avebury with the crossing of the Thames at Streatley. In former days it gave access not only to the Avebury area, but further down into Wiltshire eventually arriving at the metropolis of its day Stonehenge, on Salisbury Plain. Going in the other direction, the Thames once forded, it continued northeast up into what is now East Anglia, effectively connecting what were to become my family's roots.

Along this forty miles of green track lies a plethora of ancient sites and monuments, some highly visible whilst others are barely noticeable unless you know what to look for. But perhaps the greatest of all these antiquities is the track itself that links them all together. Although its route has changed a little in places over the years and its width too, it is to all intents and purposes very much as you would have seen it two, three, four or even five thousand years ago. The surface has become deeply rutted in some sections due in part to the passage of heavy tractors and trailers and in more recent years by four-wheel drive vehicles being driven for pleasure. But the track has always seen heavy use, albeit in different forms and at different times in its history. Being the prime arterial link at a time when metalled roads were unheard of, The Ridgeway had to carry virtually all the trade and commerce that was required to travel between the major centres it served. High quality finished flint tools from Grimes Graves flint mines in Norfolk, gold from Ireland, amber from the Baltic via the east coast and tin, from Cornwall, are but a few of the precious commodities that would have passed along its length en route for various destinations. Not heavy loads in themselves as they would to a greater degree represent the finished product, not the raw material. These were the high status goods, variously traded and bartered for or the object of gift exchange between leading lights of the day. Added to this would be the local produce in the form of grain, timber, raw flint and clay amongst others that were carried short distances to satisfy local demand, haulage presenting huge problems over any great distance. Also we should not forget the vast numbers of beasts driven on the hoof by drovers, both in the prehistoric period and right through up into the nineteenth century. It was this last use that accounts mainly for its great width, both to allow for the passage of flocks and herds and for their grazing along the way. In places you can still see the ditches and the banks that would have been surmounted by thorn bushes in order to restrict the animals and prevent them from straying into the adjoining pastoral and agricultural land. Apart from animals on the hoof, most commodities would have been carried slung over the backs of pack animals such as mules, or in panniers, but the use of wheeled carts pulled by oxen cannot be ruled out. Finally we must take into the equation the slaves and prisoners of war that would have occasionally been forced to negotiate the deep clinging mud in winter, but more likely the hard baked chalk in summer during the campaigning season. Along with the various war bands and armies of Britons, Romans, Saxons and Vikings etcetera went their horses, baggage trains and camp followers that we know tramped this route over the millennia. It is only in the last century and the new millennium that The Ridgeway has seen somewhat quieter times with tourists, walkers and the occasional farm worker going about their business to be seen. This change has come about due mainly to the development of a structured metalled road system and vehicles capable of carrying heavy loads. Prior to that, the development of the canal system in the late18th century, followed by the railways in the 19th, sounded The Ridgeway's fall from prominence as a major route.

Rather than take the more common approach of looking at The Ridgeway by way of travelling its course from east to west or in the opposite direction in order to describe the places along it, and to relate associated stories or tales, I shall instead look at sites of an archaeological nature and their environs, to illustrate something of its past and the depth of feeling and awe that The Ridgeway as a whole holds on many of us that come under its spell.

3. Avebury.

Situated as it is at the western end of The Ridgeway and not on the way to anywhere of any significance in this day and age, Avebury was for me a place of pilgrimage requiring extra effort and planning in my younger days. This was due in part to the restrictions the bus service put on. But for me the main restriction was never enough time to explore the complex of archaeological sites that surround Avebury. Now of course the journey can be made in under an hour by car from Swindon. But then, as now, a walk taking in The Ridgeway was by nature of the topography linear, not circular. So planning was crucial.

My first true experience of Avebury was on a school trip in the late 1960's. Prior to that I had passed through the ancient metropolis en route to Devizes a couple of times, but had not had the opportunity to get off the bus and explore. On those previous trips my imagination had been fired by the journey that took us along the foot of the escarpment between Wroughton and Avebury passing the rather naive figure of the Broad Hinton White Horse. This hill figure lies back off the main road a good mile and half, tucked under the crest of Hackpen Hill from which it takes its alternative name. It doesn't compare in stature, or age, to the mighty Uffington White Horse, being approximately 90ft x 90ft and carved in 1835 or 1838, depending on which account you read, on the orders of Henry Eatwell parish clerk of Broad Hinton. The latter date would seem the most likely in that it would commemorate the coronation of Queen Victoria. The above horse figure should not be confused with the one a little to the north at Broad Town of comparable age and size. Other chalk cut horse hill figures are to be seen around this part of Wiltshire, presumably inspired by the daddy of them all, Uffington, but no doubt partly by the legacy of horse breeding and training still carried on hereabouts.

During my school trip we looked at the henge at Avebury, its setting of stones, and the small museum that had been set up by Alexander Keiller, you know, him of marmalade fame. We also took in Silbury Hill and West Kennett Long Barrow. The latter I must admit to personally not seeing during that visit due in part to concern over the health of one of my teachers, but more of that later. It was this visit, skimming over the archaeology as it did, that whetted my appetite for more, very effectively fulfilling its aims presumably. Avebury itself, the village that is, sits partly encapsulated by the megalithic sarsen stones that go to make up the various stone settings. Looking at some of the houses you'll see large fragments of sarsen utilised in them. Indeed, it wasn't until 1648 that John Aubrey, after whom the Aubrey holes at Stonehenge are named, realised the importance of the stone settings and recognised the site for what it was, that being the most impressive Neolithic 'temple' complex in Britain. This identification had gone unnoticed due in part to the mediaeval buildings that made up the village incorporating the stones in their construction and the complex of hedges and fences that divided the plots, effectively preventing an overall picture from being had. Evidence of this so called clutter can be seen in photographs taken by Francis Frith in 1899 prior to full scale clearance and tidying of the site that involved the removal of many of the mediaeval and later farm buildings, cottars hovels and fences etcetera. This clearance took place in the 1930's, along with major archaeological excavations around the same time, coupled with a fair bit of 'restoration'. What we see now is nothing like the scene we would have had

80 odd years ago. Whilst there is no doubt the above actions have resulted in giving us a clearer picture of the site as a whole, it must be said that we lost a lot of the later vernacular architectural history of the village during those radical clearances.

Later visits to Avebury has helped me fill large gaps in my knowledge and understanding of just how this complex of ancient monuments and the landscape fit together. Of course we shall never know all there is to know, but as our techniques improve and our researches evolve, so will the picture. A few observations here might prompt you, the reader, to undertake some of your own research and to seek answers to questions you will undoubtedly come up with. Stand in the centre of Avebury and try to imagine the outer bank of the henge as it would have been upon completion four and a half to five thousand years ago. The bank would have stood some 6.4m high and gleamed white, the chalk taken from the ditch for its construction being freshly excavated. Between the bank and the inner ditch was a berm, a level space possibly used for access. The ditch we know had steep sides over 9m deep with a flat bottom some 4m wide, a colossal undertaking. Not a moat filled with water and a defensive bank like a medieval castle, this ditch was dry and the bank was outside the ditch. No, this was no defensive structure; the ditch was designed to keep something, or someone, in, and the bank? Possibly it was to give height to prevent unwanted eyes from seeing in, or those within from seeing out? Or do we see here an earlier equivalent of a Roman amphitheatre? Compare this site to that of the much smaller henge monument outside of Dorchester that we know the Romans reused as an amphitheatre, the outer bank serving as the support for tiers of seating. The ditch would have kept wild beasts contained and at bay. Could this site have acted as a large cattle corral? I think not. Perhaps it served as a gigantic gathering place, one in which people along with their animals congregated for feasting and law giving? Perhaps it was all of these things and much more besides. Having said all that, the origins of the name Avebury is Anglo-Saxon as its elements suggest. It's recorded in Doomsday Book as Aurebeerie, which translates as Afa's Burgh or similar, in other words old English for the stronghold belonging to Afa. This would seem to support a case for the earthworks being used for defence after all, albeit at a much later stage in the use of the site. Such a scenario cannot be ruled out, but seems very unlikely when you allow for the sheer size of the space enclosed, some 28 acres, which would make it a town by the standards of the day, not a mere thane's stronghold. It's more likely that the Saxon manor with its fortified hall stood near to where the present manor house is and that a section of the great henge earthwork acted as its defences, in which case the ditch would be effectively outside the bank where you would expect to find it. This would also account for the early church being where it is as it was formerly a monastic establishment, most likely built close to the manor house where it could be protected. If visiting Avebury try and take a look round the later manor house where hints at its earlier foundation can be seen. If time is short then at the least take in the church and the exterior of the circular stone-built dovecot nearby. The latter was once a common sight on mediaeval manorial sites, providing meat throughout the year.

Whilst pondering these facts and observations I'll throw in just a few more. What part did the 100 or so original sarsen stones of the outer circle play in all this, not to mention the two smaller inner circles of stones with their accompanying settings of stones within them? We know that the four entrances aligned roughly on the cardinal points of the compass are original from evidence gathered during excavations, and that from the western and southern of these stone rows led to Beckhampton and to 'The Sanctuary' on Overton Hill respectively. What we don't know is why? Theories and supposition abound, but hard facts are harder to come by. For me, such questions are what makes our past so interesting, makes a mystery of what to those who built them was obvious, much as in the same way we know and understand what a sports stadium is and is used for. But as is often the case, what appears to be a straightforward observation with a simple answer is in reality much more complex, rather like the site we are now discussing! A sports stadium can function at many levels for many different purposes, sports obviously, but rallies, concerts and conventions, both for leisure, religious and political purposes are other uses. They often act as venues for markets, fairs and the like, their external areas being utilised for additional parking and other activities. Do I need to say more?

Interestingly the mediaeval church in Avebury is located just outside of the henge close to the western entrance, not within its circumference as might be expected if the village had grown up within its banks. Evidence to show that the village appears to have grown fairly haphazardly and with very little regard to the monument is plainly seen in that not only was the 'Cove' partially dismantled and had buildings put up against it, but the original western entrance through the bank had dwellings built in it. These cottars' hovels stood on the undisturbed chalk that had formed a causeway across the ditch and were only removed prior to the excavations undertaken during the summer of 1938. Further evidence, if any is required, of how our later mediaeval ancestors treated the monument with distain is witnessed by the wholesale destruction by fire and water of many of the stones, others being undermined and toppled prior to being buried or broken up. This activity was being conducted as early as the first quarter of the 14th century, evidence for this coming from the discovery of the remains of a man who fell victim to one of the stones as it was toppled. He was buried where he died, no attempt being made to extricate him or to break the stone up, the stone becoming his grave slab. The contents of his purse included coins of the period along with what can only be described as surgical instruments. This last discovery has led to the man being identified as a barber-surgeon. It would appear that by the 14th century at least, the locals were not in awe of their neighbours, the stones, but were proactive in their removal and saw them as just simply a source of building stone and something to be got out of the way. In contrast, the earlier medieval inhabitants and builders of the monastic church in the Anglo-Saxon period would appear to have respected the boundaries of the former 'pagan' temple as they no doubt thought of it.

Avebury is without a shadow of a doubt the centre of a huge complex of monuments constructed in the Neolithic through into the Bronze Age, with many later monuments clustering about it. For many people it is evident that Avebury was the more important area of southern Britain than that around Stonehenge. This observation is based upon the volume, variety and age of the monuments to be found. It is also based upon the local topography and what it would have offered those living off the land at the time. Stonehenge, located on Salisbury Plain, can be a desolate place in winter with little shelter and few opportunities for gathering fuel. The same was probably true in the distant past. The Avebury area in contrast offers far greater opportunities for tree cover, building materials, shelter from gales, and also provides reasonably good light soils for cultivating with streams and seasonal winterbournes for water; all important for people rearing cattle and sowing crops. Just over two hundred years ago these same uplands would have supported similar numbers of people to thousands of years ago, quite possibly more. It's only in the intervening years that people have left the land in their droves, forced to by improvements in agriculture and the machinery that made them redundant; besides, isn't the grass always greener on the other side of the hill?

Where does The Ridgeway come into all this you may well ask? Well, as stated before, it's The Ridgeway that offered a comparatively dry route in winter, whereas in summer the lower parallel track known as the Icknield Way would have proved the more popular due to having frequent watering holes along its course. By the way, the name Icknield may well link us to the origins of the route up in Norfolk as the name is believed by some to come from Iceni, the ancient tribe that lived in the area around The Wash, the lands of Boudicca, Boadicea as she came to be known. Beyond Avebury, going south and west, the Downs form a plateau divided by narrower valleys with no obvious direct ridge routes. The traveller was made to cross these often boggy valley bottoms, inhibiting the movement of heavy traffic and large bodies of men and animals. Avebury is at the southwestern end of this particularly fine stretch of virtually unbroken chalk escarpment and connected to it by a straight piece of track known as the Herepath which leaves the village via its eastern exit. The name Herepath can be traced back to Anglo-Saxon documents. The term is said to refer to a green track, or a track used by warriors depending on which account you read. Either way, this track gives direct access to The Ridgeway, and possibly just as importantly, the origins of the stone from which the monument's megaliths are made, the grey wethers.

4. Fyfield Down and its environs.

Fyfield Down is less than two miles to the east of Avebury. At the time of my last visit, much of it was a nature reserve. The significance of this particular bit of down land lies in its abundance of stone, the residue of the former sandstone pavement that once covered the Downs overlying the softer chalk. Natural mechanical weathering by the elements over millions of years reduced this to isolated rocks much as we see today. In the five thousand years that separate us from our early Neolithic ancestors that inhabited the Downs, that same weathering has carried on but coupled with man's intervention in the form of tree clearance and intensive ploughing leading, in parts it has been estimated, to the ground surface being reduced by as much as two feet on the tops. Added to this was the practice in the 60's and 70's of grubbing out and removal of hedgerows in order to open up the fields to larger and heavier combine harvesters and tractors, which in turn allowed accelerated erosion by the wind.

Thankfully our knowledge has grown due in no small measure to archaeological research, in part leading to a reappraisal of farming practices, the damage being reduced but not entirely stopped. Fyfield Down then can be viewed as an oasis in a desert, the Downs at this point still littered with sarcens, the grey wethers shown on maps. Particularly good concentrations of sarcens can be seen in the nearby bottoms carrying streams such as Lockeridge Dene and Fyfield. It is this stone that has led to the preservation of what can best be described as pristine downland, well as near as you're likely to get. The presence of this stone has deterred farmers from cultivation of the land, sheep grazing along with rabbits being virtually the only impact, makes for good close cropped grass and light scrubby bush cover along with remnants of tree cover, ideal conditions for various species of birds, butterflies, flora and other forms of fauna.

Why this particular area was saved from wholesale clearance of stone and not turned over to agriculture remains somewhat a mystery. My own take on this is simply that this area was set aside, initially, solely for stone to be used in the building of sacred sites and monuments, perhaps because it exhibited better qualities, but more likely because it provided the easiest direct access to Avebury and its environs. Straddling the Ridgeway as it does, from here stone could be dragged and sledged downhill for the best part in either direction, thereby saving on labour and time. What remains was that presumably surplus to requirements. Incidentally, it's this area which provided the large sarcen stones used in the building of Stonehenge some twenty miles further south. Quite how such huge stones were transported over the intervening difficult terrain is anyone's guess, and we're unlikely to ever know with certainty how this was achieved.

Of the numerous archaeological monuments nearby, one in particular represents a classic form of late Neolithic/Bronze age burial site, which is the aptly named Devil's Den in Clatford Bottom. Here I have a small confession to make; I have not actually managed in all these years to visit this site in the flesh so to speak. The form taken is that of a stone chamber made up of two tall sarcens surmounted by a third making a huge capstone, a dolmen in fact. This type of burial is more commonly encountered in Cornwall or South Wales where in the latter they are known as cromlechs. Originally the chamber was covered in a mound of chalk and stone with additional stone used in plugging the gaps between the uprights giving further support to the capstone and enclosing the chamber fully. Remnants of these features are still visible. The covering mound has in part been denuded over the millennia by the weather and being ploughed, but as likely as not was reduced mainly by being used as a quarry by successive farmers.

The reason for paying particular attention to this monument is its setting and unconformity with those seen around and about it. As stated above, this type of structure is of West Country or Welsh origin primarily. Therefore the question has to be asked 'Do we have here a direct connection with the builders of Stonehenge?' This question comes about due to the smaller stones used in the construction of the horseshoe settings at Stonehenge, the so-called 'bluestones'. These bluestones are known to have come from the Preseli Mountains in South Wales and are believed to have been transported via the Bristol Channel then overland, possibly making some use of rivers to ease the effort involved. It's only a short leap from the above scenario to imagine those builders hauling the precious bluestones along the nearby river bottom of the Kennett en route for Stonehenge. Did one of their leaders die in the effort and was buried under this monument? Or did the design of this monument emulate those seen by the builders upon their travels in obtaining the bluestones? These then are just a couple of the possibilities in answering what many before me have seen as something of an enigma.

Having said all this, there is just the possibility that this monument is not the only one of its kind lying in the landscape hereabouts. When covered in its mound of chalk and grassed over, this tomb would have looked like any of the other countless round barrows dotted over the Downs. Although many of these barrows have been dug into and their contents removed, unfortunately for us these activities were often carried out in antiquity, leaving no written or illustrated records. More recently, in the nineteenth and early twentieth centuries antiquarianism led to further barrows being opened, but the lack of expertise and exuberance of the protagonists often left a lot to be desired. It has only been within the past forty or fifty years that well documented scientific excavations have been undertaken, but then sadly on very few local barrows. The maxim of recent years has been to leave well alone that which is not endangered excavation being both costly and time consuming. So it may be many more years before we can say for sure if this does in reality represent a unique monument for the area.

Meanwhile back on Fyfield Down, I must relate a little information concerning the so-called prehistoric sharpening stone to be found near to the northwest corner of the nature reserve. Lying earth-fast within a jumble of other sarcens some little way to the north of the track as you enter the reserve from Avebury is a very interesting reminder of our past. This lump of sarcen exhibits some five deeply incised parallel grooves and a shallower ovoid shaped hollow next to them on its upper surface. The highest part of this upper surface is very smooth as if from being polished. The thinking is that this was in fact used in the sharpening and grinding of axes. My question is whether it was used for stone, bronze or iron axes, or for that matter other implements? Take a closer look at the stone, that's assuming you can find it in the first place amongst so many others! It's not easy to find, but once located it jumps out at you, believe me. The ovoid hollow clearly overlays a sixth groove and part of another. This shows that the grooves affected are earlier than the hollow, but it does not prove all the remaining grooves are of the same period, although judging by their wear, depth and execution I would say on balance that they are. Here then we have evidence of two different functions or ways of working perhaps.

It is clear from the way the stone has been used that the tools being sharpened were axes or slightly convex curved bladed tools, perhaps both. As to whether these marks represent stone or metal tools, is harder to say. The grooves tend towards the sharpening of metal blades such as those used by the Anglo-Saxon's scramasax, the single edged hacking sword of the day. This would link in with the passage of troops and bring us back to the roots of the name 'Herepath'. Equally possible is the sharpening of the shorter version carried by all people in society during the early mediaeval period, men and women alike. This was basically an all-purpose knife used both for eating, no forks until the sixteenth century, and the various chores associated with farming. But neither of the above would account for the ovoid hollow. This type of mark is the direct result of a narrow blade being ground and polished in conjunction with finer sand and water to form a paste for a better finish. In this case, the profile of the hollow can leave little doubt as to the implement being ground, an axe or adze. Bearing in mind my observations concerning the grooves, I have to come to the conclusion that this is in all likelihood of mediaeval date, not prehistoric as is often claimed. Such a date would in no way be out of context as either use by many people over a short time i.e. an army, or use by a few over a long period such as a farming family would equally apply to its creation.

5. Overton Down experimental earthwork.

Finally before leaving the general area of Fyfield Down a brief mention should I feel be made of an earthwork lying to the east of The Ridgeway, a little to the north of the entrance to the nature reserve. Here can be seen a stretch of bank and ditch some twenty-one metres in length, enclosed by fencing at the time of my last visit around 1972! This is no prehistoric monument fenced off to protect it from the likes of you or I, no this was built in 1960 as part of a scientific project looking into the natural erosion of such manmade features found around the country. Built under strict controls and to specific criteria, this earthwork recreates the technology and design used in the construction of prehistoric earthworks. Encapsulated within the structure and buried about it are various modern 'artefacts' replicating those found associated with such features; organic fragments of bone, leather, wood and inorganic potsherds and discs along with flint flakes and implements. The study is designed to extend over some 128 years with periodic sampling to be undertaken as part of the program. Additional to this site is another at Wareham in Dorset, built in 1963, but here the conditions are greatly different, sandy heath-land. The monitoring and sampling of these sites will help to give a valuable insight into the degradation of buried objects, their movement within such structures and the breakdown of the structures themselves. This in turn will help in producing models from which projections and various other calculations might be made. Two major factors that will affect the results, and will be built into the study, will be the non-intervention of grazing animals and the passage of human feet due to the fencing. Another factor that will have played a greater part in the undermining and erosion of many earthworks in the last nine hundred years or so will have been the introduction of rabbits by the Normans!

To highlight just how important such research might be in our understanding of earthworks and their deterioration, a walk across The Ridgeway to a point on the Herepath overlooking Monkton Down will not go amiss. It's important that you undertake this next exercise either in the early morning or late afternoon, at least when the sun is low in the sky, be it this site or any other. Looking down and across to the foot of the escarpment below the Down will, if the conditions are right, reveal a complex of linear overlapping lines. These are the feint traces of a settlement along with its associated fields and paddocks. I first saw this literally highlighted by a low sun, the feint earthworks casting shadows. On that occasion I was using an old 1961 edition 1" to the mile ordnance survey map, which failed to show this site, so my amazement was even more intensified. The same effect is often to be got after a sprinkling of snow. This is the next best thing to obtaining an aerial photograph. Similar results can be had during a drought when the parched conditions show up buried ditches and walls caused by the effects of water availability on any crops growing above. So, even if an earthwork has become virtually ploughed out or levelled for whatever reason, there is often the chance that it will become visible under the right conditions and if viewed by someone with a trained eye!

Now take a look in the opposite direction and hopefully you will be in the right location to make out a couple of mounds on Avebury Down, possibly covered in beech trees. These are some of the round barrows so prolific in this area and thought by some to cluster round Avebury and placed on the skyline so as to be seen from the valley floor, possibly to mark outer boundaries of land holdings. When viewed from the same level it becomes apparent that many of these barrows are located below the crest of the ridges, thereby removing the obstruction caused by the convex profile making it possible for them to be seen from the lower ground. This does indeed add weight to the former theory, suggesting that the upper slopes of the downs might have been given over to the ancestors so that they could look out over the living, giving a sense of protection and security of land tenure etcetera. This type of thinking can only go some way towards understanding these monuments and how they fitted into the landscape. Unfortunately we shall never know what really drove the builders of such monuments to place them where they did, or why they practised the varied burial rites evident. Perhaps at the end of the day it might be no more than changing fashions, much the same as we can see within our present society. By the way beech, or Scots pines, planted on many of the earthworks in particular the small enclosures appear to be a comparatively recent phenomenon. Often the landed gentry undertook such plantings in the 18th and 19th centuries to provide shelter for game and to enhance the view. This can be seen as gentrification of the landscape and in some cases formed part of an elaborate plan to reproduce their version of Arcadia.

6. The Ridgeway's terminus and beyond.

Overton Hill sees the terminus of the section of The Ridgeway under review. It's here that the chalk escarpment is cut by the headwaters of the river Kennett before the route ascends the opposite hill making its way due south towards the heartland of Salisbury Plain but not before it's barred, some two mile further on, by the much later linear earthwork known as the Wansdyke. The Wansdyke is something of an enigma. Built of chalk and earth with a ditch to the north backed by an impressive bank which in its heyday would no doubt have been surmounted by a timber palisade, or more likely a stout thorny hedge, this presented quite an obstacle to anyone wanting to move freely along The Ridgeway. When viewed on a present day map, it will be seen that the Wansdyke runs basically east to west. It's thought it started in the vicinity of Inkpen a little to the south east of Hungerford and ran some fifty miles to a point on the Bristol Channel around Portishead. Obviously this was no minor defence work or cattle management scheme, but more likely part of a complex strategic line of defences raised to protect early post-Roman lands in the face of a direct Saxon threat. That threat would seem to be viewed as coming from the Thames Valley at a time when kingdoms were being moulded prior to the formation of a united England. As such, Wansdyke might be viewed as somewhat akin to Offa's Dyke or even the earlier walls constructed under the orders of the emperors Hadrian and Antoninus Pius. One wonders as to how successful such a construction was, not very judging by the ebb and flow of armies according to the writings of the Venerable Bede. Still that's another story.

For those of you who decide to undertake an exploration of this impressive monument to man's attempt at control of his fellow man's movements, a word of caution. For much of its course the earthwork traverses open downland in this part of the country with only short stretches accompanied by public footpaths. Field boundaries along with parish and county boundaries are also to be found aligned with it making for many obstacles in the form of wire fences and sometimes thick impenetrable undergrowth. In other areas along its length it runs through lush farmland and woodland, the latter providing yet another challenge to navigation and freedom of passage. Where the Wansdyke runs through Savernake Forest however, the route is easier to follow under the more open broadleaved canopy. Indeed I well remember making my way west along the earthwork during such an endeavour to follow its course from Marlborough to Morgan's Hill a little to the south of Cherhill with its White Horse figure. My way was clearly defined through the forest for some distance on that occasion due to the earthwork being carpeted in bluebells. It was as if someone had laid out a blue carpet for me, one that took a sinuous course dictated by the terrain.

Wansdyke takes its name from the Norse god Woden as does many other similar earthworks named Grim, another name for Woden, of Saxon origin. Popular belief has it such lengths of early earthworks were given this name by the Saxons who believed them to be magical and therefore attributed them to Woden. This implies they are older than the Saxon invaders and immigrants and represented something within their new landscape that required being identified, something alien to them. That theory was strongly contested in the sixties and seventies by academics, historians and archaeologists alike, and still is by many. My own thinking is that we should see this name being applied by the Saxons to earlier and contemporary earthworks as a form of dedication and in praise of their god Woden as they progressed through the land and claimed fresh territory. In no way do I think the Saxons were in awe of these earthworks or mystified by their creation. They after all were very familiar with building such defences in their own homelands, were equally aware of them within the late Roman world on the Continent, and built similar earthworks themselves here. The fact is that we only have Anglo-Saxon literature to go on as mentioned above, no Roman sources remain, written evidence first making its appearance once England as we know it has been fully colonised. In other words, the victors pass on their achievements and take the credit for such features within the landscape.

Now back to our terminus of The Ridgeway on Overton Hill. Here is to be found the Neolithic site known as The Sanctuary. This site is linked to Avebury by the Kennett Avenue, a linear alignment of paired sarcen stones running for over a mile and giving weight to theories of The Sanctuary being a temple forming part of a complex, with its processional way making it perhaps of greater importance than Avebury itself. What we see here today is somewhat uninspiring and lacks the wow factor of Avebury or Silbury Hill, but nether the less must be taken into the equation and seen for what it is, the all but lost site of a stone monument (destroyed in 1724) far more involved and important than we are ever likely to know. Unfortunately concrete posts marking the former positions of stones, and earlier wooden posts, do nothing to convey a sense of power, importance or atmosphere, and like its sister monument Woodhenge near Stonehenge, fails to impress and hold the imagination. At the time of my visits the forlorn looking greasy spoon transport cafe over the road didn't exactly help matters either!

The A4 at this point blots the landscape and is an added danger to proceeding south along The Ridgeway. In many ways it can be compared to the road driven through the landscape by the Romans, just a little to the north. This road can barely be seen on the ground now as it crosses The Ridgeway clipping a barrow in the process. But in its day this road, orientated west to east, linking Bath with Silchester would have made a bold statement to the local non-Roman population. That statement was 'we're here to stay, so don't mess with us'. Look at your map and you'll see how this very road allowed quick movement of troops and commodities between the smaller Roman towns of Verlvcio, Sandy Lane and Cvnetio, Mildenhall. This brought power and commerce, the two main factors in determining the fate of Britain for some four hundred years. Any significance or vestiges of the importance that The Sanctuary along with Avebury might have retained at the arrival of the Romans will have been quickly dashed I feel sure. No doubt the tribal leaders did well under the new regime, whilst the average Brit working on the land probably noticed very little difference initially. Those that succumbed to the Roman way of life and moved into the newly established towns would have prospered in the long run, passing trade and wider markets offering commercial opportunities, the road proving the essential link. This same road, or rather the present A4, takes us to our next site.

7. Silbury Hill and West Kennett long barrow.

Silbury Hill is the largest prehistoric manmade mound, at 130ft high, in Europe, or so the authors of the numerous books on archaeology would have us believe. I must admit to not being able to refute this claim, but wonder if it really can be true. That aside, you cannot fail to be impressed with such a feat of engineering, a mass of earth and chalk scraped up and dug from its surrounding ditch that is contemporary with the earliest pyramids of ancient Egypt. Dating is always problematical, but a date of around circa 4,750 years before the present is now accepted. The cone shaped profile and level top does little to betray the complexity of the structure. Buried within are walls made from chalk blocks providing a tiered wedding cake type construction with three phases discernable; at least that is what the evidence led us to believe from the numerous excavations carried out over the past two hundred years or so up until 2000, more of this later. These excavations have consisted of tunneling into the mound from its sides and base, and sinking a shaft from the summit with the objective primarily to find evidence of a central burial chamber. Additional to the above, trenches have been opened on the summit and around its base in the past. To date no burial has been found, or the slightest hint of one, although it is highly probable that the first phase consisted of a conventional round barrow. The shaft sunk from the top of the mound in 1776 would almost certainly have destroyed any central burial! My own recollections are of the tunnel driven into the hill along with associated excavations under the auspices of the BBC and televised in the Chronicle series back in the late sixties. I well remember travelling out to Silbury from Swindon on the school trip mentioned previously. Needless to say nothing was to be seen, apart that is from all the television paraphernalia which at the time was exciting in itself. These were the early days of televised popular archaeology as presented by such notable celebrities as Magnus Magnusson, when live outside broadcasts were in their infancy. This was years before the days of Time Team when to set up a shot involved a military type operation, with equipment that filled every available space. Many people like myself, were inspired by those early television programs and went on to take up archaeology as a career.

In May 2000 subsidence of the 1776 shaft sunk into the hill from the top caused a stir, and the opportunity to undertake further excavations on the summit. Subsequent excavations, consolidation and research along with a seismic survey showed this is not the first time such an event had taken place. On possibly two previous occasions back in the 1920's and 30's remedial measures had been taken to fill a hole. With the benefit of new technology we can now be fairly certain that there are no more voids in the shaft, although the survey did show some collapse of the 1969 tunnel. But the survey also showed more. The hill appears to have been built not using a tiered type construction as previously suggested, but to have been raised utilising a spiral ramp running anti-clockwise. This ramp in turn was linked to radiating walls, which were themselves tied together with straight stretches of wall. The whole would look akin to a three-dimensional spider's web if the overlying earth and chalk skin were peeled away. This sequence of events was closely parallel to a similar but less dramatic occurrence on the site of the bakery within the Norman castle at Old Sarum, the precursor to Salisbury. On that occasion, in summer 1999, a backfilled mediaeval well shaft sunk through the chalk of the hill subsided. I was a part of the team from Wessex Archaeology to carry out the excavation and consolidation for English Heritage.

During another visit to Silbury I have seen the base of the hill surrounded by floodwaters. This is a fairly common occurrence. In such circumstances the hill resembles an enormous Norman motte surrounded by its moat, indeed, such a description might not be so very far off the mark. Whilst excavating the summit of the hill in 1969 Richard Atkinson records evidence of the top terrace having been "revetted by timber secured with iron nails." Dating evidence came from a farthing, a quarter cut from a silver penny of Aethelred 11 minted in 1010AD, the small change of the day, and encapsulated within the stratigraphy. Atkinson believes this along with other evidence from his excavations shows that Silbury Hill was fortified in the late Saxon period, most likely in response to the Danish raids of that period. Alternatively this might represent a Danish stronghold or even an early timber 'keep' erected on the top of the hill prior to the Norman invasion, or soon after. One thing that Atkinson's excavations proved was that rubbish of early fourth century date, from a Roman settlement nearby, filled the ditch. That coupled with the first century Roman road that is aligned on the hill, and literally bends to go round its base, proves the hill's prehistoric date. This last fact though has never really been in question.

That school trip back in 1968 took in not only Silbury Hill but also both Avebury and West Kennett long barrow. The BBC made Silbury Hill at that time accessible via a new footpath from Avebury along with parking, put in place as part of the planning consent. This meant a fairly long walk, but kept visitors off the A4 which in those days was far busier as it was just prior to the construction of the M4 which has since greatly reduced the traffic. The path to the top of Silbury was very narrow and round its way up and around with very little room for manoeuvre. Imagine a hoard of school kids then, racing to be at the top first. I did not envy my teachers their task but somehow they got us up and down again with no injuries. Mind you, it was not without some cost. After our inspection of Silbury we moved on to view West Kennett long barrow. This involved having to walk alongside the A4 for something like 300yds in order to access the path that leads up the hill on which the barrow sits. Just a hundred yards or so along the path it kinks to go round a field, here my elderly science teacher decided enough was enough and sat down under the shade of a tree. The decision was made that the school party would proceed after I had volunteered to stay with 'Sir' and await their return. At the time I had no idea what I was missing. Some thirty minutes later my 'classmates' returned to say they had just been into a cave and seen fantastic wall paintings and skeletons! Well my jaw dropped and I was green with envy. Only later was I to learn of their embellishments, but at the time I felt thoroughly cheated. Why? Well during that wait 'Sir' recovered with a cup of tea from his thermos, and a fag!

West Kennett is a site not to be missed if possible, it and those already described if you're of the same persuasion as me, a complete archaeolgicalolic. Even if you're not, I would still recommend the excursion as part of a foray of the Avebury area. The barrow sits on the crest of the hill; its coffin shaped mound extending to some 330ft making it one of the longest such mounds in the country. The entrance is through a blanking facade at its eastern end made of sarcen megaliths, originally put up to finally close the burial chambers off from the outside world. This sealing of the tomb took place some 4,300 years ago, well before many of the neighbouring monuments were built and around 1,300 years after its original construction. Enter the tomb proper and you enter another world, the world of the dead. Don't let this last remark fool you though, as it's been shown that the tomb was often opened between internments, some of the bones being removed for unknown purposes and then re-deposited, others showing signs of having been left in the open air prior to deposition presumably to be de-fleshed by birds and the like. Some forty-six humans were represented, but not all their bones accounted for. So whilst the tomb did in deed act as a repository for the dead, those no doubt of the royal bloodline or similar standing within the community, it appears to have also served as a place of feasting, celebration, possibly meditation and initiation and maybe all these. We may be seeing here the equivalent of a parish church, possibly even a cathedral of the mediaeval period.

The interior of the tomb is indeed cave-like; a long central passage with chambers off each side leads to a single chamber at the rear. Where a huge sarcen capstone once acted as the ceiling is now an opaque glass panel to admit subdued natural daylight. This was inserted after the excavations in the mid 50's as part of the reconstruction of the monument. Even so, a magical atmosphere pervades the place. Not the cheap touristy Disney type, but a sense of the unknown, of deep antiquity, of human existence, that's always provided you get the place to yourself and there's not the inevitable stench from stale urine in high summer, often the result of parents allowing their youngsters to relieve themselves after being taken short. If these last observations offend, or put you off, don't let them. This is a fact of life when exploring such out of the way sites, even some in busy public places! To avoid the above, try visiting out of season, early spring or autumn can be ideal. Failing that, go early morning when the low light can add another dimension to the quality of your visit. A torch is handy for seeing into some of the darker corners and to highlight the sharpening and polishing marks left by stone axes, believed to represent part of the original construction where timber was required for levers and props. Oh, and to set the record straight, there are no genuine wall paintings, or skeletons! You might see the odd modern graffito, or as I did on a recent visit, candles and offerings of flowers and the like, made to unknown gods by unknown individuals.

I have used quite a bit of space in writing about Avebury and its environs, mainly because of the national importance that this area plays in our pre-historic past. Unfortunately I have also had to leave a lot unsaid, mention of the recent work around the Beckhampton stones, the East Kennett long barrow and the multitude of other sites, but perhaps most important of all Windmill Hill and its causewayed camp. For further archaeological and historical information concerning these sites there are countless guides and academic publications available, many of which are available in the museum in Avebury. But as a final word before leaving what I consider was the ancient metropolis of Britain let me add this. No visit to Avebury is really complete without going into the Red Lion Inn. Not only will you find a pleasant country pub but an unexpected feature that such a building occasionally hides. Within the present establishment is a stone lined well, lit discreetly and acting as a talking point. The significance of this feature is that access to fresh water was at a premium to our forebears and more recent ancestors on the dry chalk uplands hereabouts. This was a coaching inn; the well when originally sunk was in the yard. The inn expanded incorporating the well as times proved good, no doubt in part due to tourism thanks to the discoveries made by Aubrey back in 1648.

8. Barbury Castle.

Barbury is the most southern fort in a chain forming a defensive line along The Ridgeway. I say fort as opposed to castle as the layout of these tremendous earthworks clearly belong to defended enclosures quite unlike the later mediaeval castles with stone towers and encircling walls. The earliest mediaeval castles were on the whole much smaller than what we have here. Earth mottes, that's the artificial mound rather like an upturned pudding bowl as depicted in the Bayeux Tapestry, put up to act as a platform for a fighting tower usually placed within a palisade all made of stout timbers were the norm. These in turn were often as not enclosed by a ditch and an outer area again enclosed by a timber palisade and ditch, the bailey. With time and changing needs, these timber fortifications were replaced with stone, enlarged, made more intricate and became permanent features within the landscape, that is, if the said castle was still required. Just occasionally a castle might be abandoned and slighted shortly after erection due to hostility, but more often than not due to being badly sited in the first place. Such a site that never got beyond the earthwork and timber stage is a little over three miles to the northwest and known as Binknoll Castle. A foray down onto the large terrace like plain laid out below Barbury to look at this site is well worth the effort. Binknoll sits atop the lip of a smaller parallel escarpment giving panoramic views to the north and Wootton Bassett (now given the Royal prefix). It's a magical place, the castle earthworks sitting as it does amongst mature woods clinging to the escarpment, the last vestiges of once vast expanses of managed woodland, the very woods that would no doubt have furnished the timber for the palisades that encircled Barbury. Such mottes often survive in the fields in isolation, their surrounding earthworks having been ploughed flat whilst others are to be found forming features within the landscaped grounds of country houses, larger castles and ecclesiastical sites. Examples of these are to be seen at Christchurch Priory in Dorset, within the city walls of Southampton, Lewis Castle in West Sussex and nearer to home, Marlborough College. Some care is needed in identification with the last two sites, as there are some doubts as to their original purpose. Lewis boasts two mottes within the curtilage of the castle one surmounted by a shell keep of stone, the other now a grassy mound. A third 'motte' is to be seen on the valley floor, presumably the earliest, guarding the crossing of the river Ouse, incidentally the Celtic for water! Quite how all these relate to each other is complex to say the least. In the case of Marlborough College, here we have a prehistoric mound rather akin to Silbury Hill, recent scientific research proving its earlier origins. The Normans utilized the existing mound and turned it into a motte that once guarded the river crossing of the Kennett and the market town that grew up beneath it, at the same time declaring its secular power by overshadowing the churches below. Later landscaping in the post-mediaeval period was to change its profile in much the same way as those at Christchurch Priory and Southampton.

Having gone off at a tangent, I shall now return to Barbury. Barbury Castle lies astride The Ridgeway proper. A lower track to the north skirting the bottom of the hill will have served in the summer effectively bypassing Barbury for anyone heading for Liddington, Barbury's sister fort to the east. Between them these two forts controlled the passage of anyone approaching from the north, and later overlooked the important Roman road previously referred to. Well that is what one would assume, but I have no doubt that at the time the Romans drove their road through this neck of the woods the locals held no fear for them. All evidence points to Barbury along with the other forts as being of pre-Roman date in construction, Iron Age with a hint of late Bronze Age origins say between two to three thousand years old. They strategically bar access along The Ridgeway thereby controlling the passage of enemy forces, but more importantly the trade goods that undoubtedly were transported along its entire route. Whoever held these forts held great power over commerce and the everyday lives of the people living within their shadow. As an example of this you only need to look at the discovery of a cache of twelve bronze cauldrons (known as the Chiseldon cauldrons) dating from the iron-age and excavated near to the fort in 2004. This find represents collective wealth, on a par with anything found throughout Europe. Approach Barbury from the southwest and you're faced with the ramparts of the fort atop the crest of the hill towering above you. Approach from the east and the story is somewhat different. Here the track follows the top of the Downs, the fort actually appearing slightly below the level of the ridge. But from whichever direction you approach, there's no mistaking the huge banks and ditches that go to make up the in-depth defences of this fort.

Imagine if you can the banks of the fort when newly constructed, they would have shone white in the sun the glare on a fine day may well have formed part of a built-in design factor. You would have seen the ramparts from miles away and to attack them without the benefit of 'shades' would have proved pure purgatory. To have lived within the ramparts was another thing, the glare no doubt reduced by grass cover on the inner face of the bank and the interior. Stand within the earthworks and your view out is severely curtailed by the bank towards the north and east. Put a ten foot (two to three metres) high timber palisade on the bank for good measure and the sense of enclosure would become even greater. That said the area enclosed, at around eleven and a half acres, along with the fall in level towards the south and west precludes any feeling of claustrophobia. Now go a step further; imagine clusters of round houses, their conical thatched roofs rising to points some thirty feet (nine metres) above the ground, their daubed walls, without windows, possibly brightly painted with symbols. The entrances, with their porches, will likewise have been highly adorned in all probability and predominantly faced the southeast. This layout, often as not, is to be seen throughout the country as it not only admitted the rays from the early morning sun to light the working and living areas within, but also afforded protection against the prevailing wind. In the entrances shallow scoops, formed by chickens making dust baths whilst sharing the warmth from the fire within, might have had to be negotiated!

Here and there would be little fenced paddocks and yards for securing livestock, horses and even areas for parking chariots. Too farfetched do you think? Well I don't think so as the Downs hereabouts would have provided ideal topography for the use of chariots and ponies would need to be corralled. Perhaps some two thousand years ago your eye would have been drawn to a gathering of women talking excitedly and carrying an assortment of large jars, leather vessels, wood and bronze buckets. This would be a party setting out for the springs located below the ramparts of the fort in order to fetch drinking water, a quarter or a half-mile distant. If a well existed within the fort, then in all probability its use would be reserved for the leading family and their retainers, or perhaps the fighting elite. This was the scenario, well documented, a thousand years later within the inner ward of the Norman castle at Old Sarum, Salisbury, itself a reused Iron Age fort located in a similar topographical position to that of Barbury.

Another source of water existed just outside the fort on the lower southern slopes of the hill, a dew pond, no longer cared for and therefore unusable. Such features were once commonly found in the chalk uplands of Southern Britain and provided reserves of water for man and beast alike. For those of you unfamiliar with dewponds, they are large circular shallow saucer type depressions averaging some 20 metres across. Lined with straw and puddled clay to form an impervious layer, they collected both rainwater and condensation and made ideal watering holes for animals. However, the fresh uncontaminated sweeter water from the springs dotted along the spring-line would have demanded a premium for human consumption, but could not be relied upon all year round. It therefore cannot be overemphasized as to just how important a regular water supply was to a large community in such a place. Even if you follow the thinking of many archaeologists, and others, that such forts were not in everyday use, the demand for water nevertheless would have put tremendous pressure on such a precious resource when a fort like Barbury was occupied, no matter for how short a space of time.

Barbury Castle must have seen many people pass through its earthen entrances, formerly defended by catwalks, towers and solid timber gates. Now they are less menacing with soft green downland turf carpeting rounded terminals, ideal places to lie under a vast deep blue summer sky listening to the sound of sky larks high overhead. Such thoughts conjure up childhood memories and later, poets....

Memories are born in such a place as Barbury, memories that are transferred from parent to child, uncle to nephew and between partners down the years. My first recollections of Barbury were on trips out with my parents when I would play on the slopes with them, a brother or a friend. The usual game was defenders and besiegers, which involved a lot of physical tugging and pushing, and often resulted in grazed knees and the odd bruise. But what the heck, it was fun. Out of this developed what I would like to call an early form of bungee jumping, but without the rope! The idea was that you ran along the top of the bank and launched yourself head first at speed down into the ditch turning a somersault as you went. If you judged it right you landed on your bum with your feet tucked under you so that you were now in a good position to either stop and stand up, or push off into a series of further somersaults that would eventually bring you to a halt in the bottom of the ditch, feeling giddy and exulted all at once. The trick was in getting the speed right, a tad too fast and you lost control ending up in a heap, a tad too slow and you came to an undignified stop. Selecting the right bit of hill was crucial as a hawthorn or gorse bush played havoc with the trousers! I had perfected the technique at about eleven years of age when a huge contoured and terraced hill of earth had appeared in Ferndale rec. my local recreation ground near to my home in Swindon.

Not all was boisterous daring do. I have to confess to picking daisies along with my mother and making them into the inevitable daisy chain. Not really P.C. in this day and age I know, although I was connecting with my feminine side! But perhaps above all was being able to just sit on the grass and enjoy a picnic amongst glorious scenery in complete peace and quiet. From this vantage point we would also watch the military aircraft coming and going from the aerodrome at Wroughton below, now the site of the Science Museum's magnificent venue, the sound from their propellers usually carried away on the breeze. I never really questioned the existence of the airfield or what part it played in protecting our world, or blighting the lives of those who held differing views. Likewise, I never gave a thought to the military hospital, or the establishment at Burdrop that served the community as an out of the way place for psychologically affected patients. Life as a child in the mid-sixties was still comparatively sheltered from the real world, the media and news bodies curtailed by restrictive reporting and little broadcasting time on television. Most of what I remember from those times is rose tinted bright sunny days with cotton wool clouds in the sky that never seemed to obscure the sun.

As an adult I've introduced Barbury to my own children and a few selected friends. I shall never forget my youngest son, who in the mid 1990's was around eleven years of age, being absolutely dumbfounded by my acrobatics whilst demonstrating to him the art of throwing oneself off the rampart into the ditch! I would have been around forty at the time and my hair quite white. It took some encouragement getting him to join in, but once his initial fear was overcome there was no holding him back. On that occasion I was intrigued to see that The Borough of Thamesdown, or Swindon Corporation as I knew it, had enhanced access to the fort from the east, providing a fair sized parking area, toilets and well laid out paths along with information panels. Of particular amusement was the reference on these interpretation panels to the appearance of crop circles in the fields below the fort, amongst details referring to the archaeology and history of the area. This was a comparatively new phenomenon at the time with many debates, and numerous theories put forward as to their origins and significance. Terence Meaden in his book The Goddess of the Stones (1991) tried valiantly to convince us they were natural phenomena when it was quite obvious they were the work of farmers, students and pranksters out to hoodwink the general public, but even more so the lunatic fringe who saw them as messages from the gods or evidence for visitations from extraterrestrial beings and the like!

Returning swiftly to the real world; Barbury has been identified as the place where according to The Anglo-Saxon Chronicle, in 556AD, the British fought a battle against the invading Saxons, the latter led by Cynric and Ceawlin. Known as Beranburgh, the outcome of the battle is not stated, whereas normally it would be. The implication, I believe, is that the Britons at the very least forced a stalemate, maybe even won. That aside, the site of the battle is shown on the Ordnance Survey map as being just half a mile below the fort to the north, near to a small earthwork within a wood. I should like to think that the earthwork represents the temporary fortified camp of the Saxons prior to the battle, the British sallying out from their hastily refortified fort. As to the exact date and original purpose of this earthwork I don't know, but a little romanticising doesn't hurt. When standing here below the fort with the sun setting you can appreciate its banks and ditches silhouetted against the darkening sky. To the east, your left, are to be seen some of the best examples of 'Celtic Fields', the small square and rectangular fields tumbling down the lesser slopes of the escarpment. Also seen are what appear to be terraces. These are actually strip lynchets, the result of continuous ploughing along the contour of the hill resulting in the buildup of earth and chalk banks. Thought by antiquarians in Victorian times to be Iron Age, many are now known to date from the Romano-British period and some the result of later mediaeval farming.

9. Chiseldon and beyond.

Chiseldon as previously mentioned lies on the lip of the lower escarpment overlooking Swindon immediately to the north. The route of the present Ridgeway Long Distance Footpath runs to the south of the village as it makes its way towards the foot of Liddington Hill, the next large Iron Age fort if you travel from south to northeast. This is virtually the only stretch of The Ridgeway that is covered in tarmac, and at Foxhill some two miles further beyond Liddington Hill is to be found the only public house (at the time of writing) actually sitting alongside the path, that is if you discount Streatley at the extreme eastern end of The Ridgeway section under discussion.

Chiseldon Plain, as I call it, is the area of downland bounded by Chiseldon to the north and Ogbourne St. George to the south, with the hill forts of Barbury and Liddington to the west and east. To the south, west and east is the higher downland with what I (along with other purists) would describe as the true and original route of the pre-historic Ridgeway running along the top of the escarpment. This escarpment varies in height, rising between three to four hundred feet above the floor of the plain. Running from north to south on the line of the Roman road, effectively dividing the plain in two is the A345. To the west of the road is sprawled two 'camps'. These drab looking concentrations of military married quarters and other buildings were for me as a youth places of mystery and gave this whole area a 'Bermuda Triangle' feeling. They still do! My experience of these camps was restricted to passing by on the A345, or meandering through them on the bus en route to Salisbury.

Smeathe's Ridge bounds Chiseldon Plain to the west and gives direct access from Barbury Castle along its crest to Ogbourne St. George. The walk along this ridge is nothing short of fantastic on a glorious summer's day, dropping down as it does into Ogbourne St. George where you skirt the army camp to the south before emerging into the village proper. Here the chalk stream widens to become the River Og flowing south to Marlborough where it joins the Kennet. To the south is Southend, a tiny cluster of half-timbered houses. To the north is what used to be known as Swindon Golf Club, now that title is given to the new course at Coate on the outskirts of Swindon. It was on the stretch of road that climbs up from the village onto Poulton Downs and over to Mildenhall, that I had my first experience of getting behind the wheel of a car. The tarmac road gives way to a farm track as it crests the down before dropping to the site of the Roman town of Cunetio, Mildenhall. Close by is the now derelict Swindon to Marlborough railway line. I once attempted to walk its course through the Chiseldon Plain to Marlborough. My efforts were frustrated by dismantled bridges, barbed wire and undergrowth, but I won through in the end with the odd detour.

The eastern flank of Chiseldon Plain is bordered by Round Hill Downs, which in turn gives way to Whitefield Hill and eventually Liddington Hill. Just above Round Hill Downs and bordering the north side of Aldbourne Chase is the site of the village of Snap. Walk across the close cropped grass that covers the undulations marking the former houses, outbuildings and paddocks, and you may be forgiven for thinking this is another deserted mediaeval village, DMV, the outcome of a failed water supply or the Black Death, the plague. Well you'd be wrong. Its inhabitants vacated Snap as recently as the late 19th century in order that sheep could have the run of the hill. Henry Wilson, a Ramsbury butcher, was cashing in on the demand for meat from the increasing populations of the industrial centres like Swindon. This was in effect a Highland Clearance in lowland Britain! Interestingly earlier 18th and 19th century clearances of part or even whole villages are well documented, usually to provide the landowner with a better view from their newly built big house, for example Milton Abbas in Dorset and Stourhead here in Wiltshire. What seems particularly ironic in this case is that the name of the village comes from Old Scandinavian, Viking, meaning 'poor pasture'!

Just a little north of Snap is Upper Upham. This is the site of a large Romano-British settlement, the buildings along with their associated fields making for extensive earthworks. Below the escarpment facing Chiseldon Plain are a series of ditches traversing the contours, these earthworks are clearly seen from the A345. In all probability they represent land management associated with the control of cattle in the Iron Age and later into the Romano-British period. At the end of these earthworks is the Iron Age fort atop Liddington Hill. It doesn't take much thinking to see the connection. It's here that we rejoin The Ridgeway, but in antiquity this would most likely have proved to be the preferred route as it provided grazing and was drier underfoot. This ridge effectively divides the Chiseldon Plain from the Wanborough Plain and the narrow valley leading to Aldbourne. Aldbourne is one of at least three places I know of associated with the origins of the story relating to the name Moonraker given to Wiltshire locals; the others are Bishop Cannings and Devizes. See below for my take of the Moonraker story.

Liddington Hill, the sister fortress to Barbury, overlooks Chiseldon Plain and the lower course of the present Ridgeway. Like Barbury it effectively controlled the passage of people and animals along this ancient route. At just 90ft short of the thousand-foot mark, this makes it the highest point on The Ridgeway. Although not so impressive as the earthworks surrounding Barbury, it's the close proximity to the lower escarpment giving the feeling of being in a loftier position that makes the location that bit more dramatic. The views out over the Vale of White Horse and the Thames basin are quite spectacular on a clear day. It's to here that the young Richard Jefferies often came, later well known as the Wiltshire poet and writer, partly to escape the tensions in the family home at Coate Farm, but also to drink in the atmosphere of the open Downs. Jefferies makes an ideal link with the last quarter of the Victorian age about which he wrote with such knowledge and conviction. Not only covering the agricultural developments and natural history scene during this period, Jefferies also ventured into the politics and economics of the day. A man in many ways far in advance of his time, as the saying goes Jefferies is commemorated here within the defences of Liddington Castle by an inscribed stone. Look out from this spot to the northwest now and the scene will have changed dramatically since Jefferies days. Below now runs the M4 Motorway, beyond that stretches Thamesdown, Swindon with its outlying areas once displaying individual characteristics. All now have become an entangled mass, a sprawling conglomeration of housing, offices, light industry, roads and yet more roads. To pick out Coate Farm and Day House Lane with its former brick works and remains of a stone circle, requires more than just the naked eye, but more the eye of faith!

My ancestors worked, lived, played and died in the area below my feet; Wanborough, Chiseldon, Wroughton, Walcot, Stratton St. Margaret and Swindon. Contemporaries of Richard Jefferies, who was born into the landed classes, the lower gentry, my ancestors were of the working class that toiled in the fields, latterly in the 'factory' the Great Western Railway workshops. Earlier still, going back some three hundred and fifty years, my ancestors were still working the land, but to the north and west of Swindon in Minety and Leigh.

Directly below Liddington Castle lies Badbury, formerly the name ascribed to Liddington Castle itself, as seen on maps of 1610 and 1695 by John Speed and Robert Morden respectively. It's believed by some that Badbury Hill (Baydon Hill by others) was the site of the famous victory associated with the legendary Arthur over the Saxons known as the battle of Mons Badonicus, sometime around the end of the fifth century AD. Interestingly, just a little to the northwest lies Badbury Wick, the Wick element often indicating a Roman origin. In 1969-70, when the M4 Motorway was being constructed, workmen came across a few bronze coins of Roman date. Word got out, but not before a large area was disturbed in a hunt for more coins. In those days when emergency archaeology was required fast, the local amateur archaeological group was generally called out to assist the County Archaeologist, or local museum curator. In this case I formed part of that response as a member of SAARG, the Swindon Area Archaeology Research Group. What we found was the remains of a bath wing incorporating a plunge bath and a fragment of a further wing that had been a substantial Roman villa. Unfortunately the motorway construction had been driven right through the main body of the villa, effectively obliterating it. Excavations were carried out over many weekends, the results being recorded prior to the site being covered with breathable sheeting and then backfilled with a layer of sand prior to being landscaped into the embankment of the motorway. It's ironic really that the villa had originally been sited where it was to take full advantage of the Roman road that had been driven through earlier British tribal lands; now in turn it had been trashed to accommodate a new breed of road, the Motorway. Badbury is now edged by the M4 Motorway, cutting its way through the chalk of the Downs, hidden from view for the best part, all but from our present vantage point!

10. The Wiltshire 'Moonraker'.

For those of you unfamiliar with the Moonraker story, the nickname by which Wiltshire folk are known, it goes something like this. Back in the 18th and early 19th centuries when smuggling was rife, due to the high tax imposed on certain foreign luxury goods partly as a result of Napoleon's activities, large bodies of men were to be seen transporting contraband across country on mules and in carts by night. You know the sort of thing, "Watch the wall my darling while the gentlemen go by". But for many rural folk this was no idyllic life style, but a case of needs must to put food on the table. Well on one bright moonlit night with clouds scurrying across the sky, such a band of smugglers were passing through Aldbourne when news was brought to them that a party of excise men was approaching and that their route was blocked. In haste the smugglers unhitched their ponies and abandoned the slow moving carts loaded with casks of brandy and other spirits, calling upon a couple of locals to hide the load, leaving them a flagon of cider for their pains. They then took to the hills, the plan being to return later once the heat was off. That left George and his mate in something of a dilemma. What was to be done with the contraband? To be caught in possession of illegal spirits would bring the death penalty, at the very least transportation to the colonies for life! To just abandon the casks and flee would leave them open to the revenge of the smugglers. They were what you might say 'caught between a rock and a hard place'.

Without further ado, panicking at their plight, George indicated to his mate that they heave the casks into the village pond lashed together with cargo netting and weighted down with stones. This done the casks floated just below the surface of the pond where they were invisible to the eye. They had only just finished and started on the cider when they heard the thunder of horses' hooves and many shapes loomed up out of the night; the excise men were upon them. Sweating with their exertions, George and mate stood silent by the side of the pond as the excise men stopped nearby. The officer in charge rode forward and looked down at the pair from his dapple-grey steed. "Has a party of men passed this way?" As he questioned them his sergeant drew up alongside caressing his sabre in a menacing fashion, leaving them in no doubt as to what would happen to them if they gave any trouble, or failed to cooperate. George looked up at the officer from under his broad brimmed felt hat whilst at the same time clutching the cider flagon; his mate, silent beside him, stared down at his bare feet. Both trembled. "Yes Sir, there be lots of um, they went that way not ten minutes past" George blurted out as he pointed to the east. The officer eyed George up and down. George felt himself shrink and at the same time come out in an additional cold sweat to add to his misery. "Were they leading many laden pack animals?" the officer quizzed. "Yes Sir, nose t' tail they be and staggering under the weight" replied George. "Good" said the officer smiling to him-self as he turned to his sergeant, "Now we have them, they will not get far so loaded. Time is on our side, let the horses drink".

George and mate now sank to the ground and sat there whilst the excise men watered their horses. The next few minutes seemed like an eternity. "Why does your mate no speak up? Cat got his tongue?" The sergeant stood over George, sabre in hand. "He ain't got any tongue, he be dumber and drunker than me". George looked up, at the same time he jabbed his mate in the side with his elbow and gave the sergeant a broad toothless grin. His mate held back from calling out in pain and bursting forth with a tirade of expletives. The sergeant knelt beside George and went to take the cider flagon from him, but catching a whiff of his breath, thought better of it! Rising back to his feet the sergeant turned and walked away muttering to himself, 'Trust me to come across the village drunk and the village mute'!

A moment later and the officer called to his men, "To horse, to horse. Within the hour we shall have our prey". Off they rode into the night leaving George and mate alone once more with their problem. Hurriedly the two men began to haul on the ropes securing the casks. With the use of a handcart they intended transferring the contraband to a disused limekiln nearby. As they grappled with the casks one broke away, floated to the surface and began to drift into deeper water. Taking a hay rake George waded in after the cask and was in the middle of retrieving it when to his horror up rode the sergeant accompanied by two troopers. There stood George up to his waist in water, his mate not far away with water lapping his knees. "And what is it you're about now?" demanded the sergeant, whose officer had had a niggling doubt and ordered him to return hoping to catch George and mate out. "What us Sir?" "Yes you, you nincompoops". George looked to his mate for inspiration, but not finding any he gazed at the rake in his hand, speechless. Moments passed in silence broken only by the snort of the sergeant's mount. It was then that George realised that the sergeant couldn't see the cask beneath the head of the rake and that it in turn was just a foot or so from the full moon's reflection that glistened brightly on the surface of the water. "Ah, I be a retrieving this here cheese as fallen into pond". With that George made great play of extending the rake and drawing it back and forth across the moon's reflection, all the while holding the cask down below the surface of the water. The sergeant looked on sternly, fingering his sabre. George played out the scene for all he was worth, looking round to his mate and calling him to his assistance as he couldn't seem to catch the 'cheese'. Slowly the sergeant's face turned to one of amusement, a broad smile dismissing the antics of George and mate as the actions of buffoons. Wheeling his mount round the sergeant called the troopers to follow as he galloped off to rejoin his unit muttering to himself, 'Trust me to come across not only the village drunk and the village mute, but the village idiots too. Just wait to the Captain hears about this, moon raking indeed'.

The contraband retrieved and stashed in its new hiding place, George and mate now sat back and emptied the cider flagon. The following night a group of dark shadowy figures were to be seen removing the casks from the lime kiln, two of which were left in the safe keeping of George and mate by way of thanks and to keep them quiet. The essence of this story is don't be fooled by Wiltshire folk, we ain't as daft as we looks! Of course we could go on to other nicknames applied to so called local Wiltshire bumpkins, turnip or Swede bashers for instance, but that's another story!

11. Wayland's Smithy.

Wayland's Smithy lies just a few yards off the Ridgeway a little over a mile southwest of Whitehorse Hill. Access is via The Ridgeway, the nearest car parking being the Whitehorse Hill car park or alongside the B400 from Ashbury to Lambourne. Remember, the Ridgeway is designated as a by-way, which whilst you would be perfectly within your rights to use your car, in practise this would be very unwise due to the rutted nature of the track and deep mud in wet conditions. My advice to anyone using The Ridgeway is to walk. Four wheel drive vehicles really should only be used by those farming the land hereabouts. I say this for three good reasons. First is to reduce any undue wear to the track so as to leave it as passable as is possible for the maximum range of users on foot, horseback or bicycle. Secondly, this is a working environment, which means that a car stuck in the mud might prevent a farmer going about his daily business. Third is the damage to the environment and unseen archaeological deposits that often results from unnecessary use by powered vehicles. Pet talk over, I'll proceed.

Most people know that Wayland's Smithy is a Neolithic chambered long barrow which places it around five thousand seven hundred years before the present. What the casual observer doesn't necessarily appreciate is that it consists of two monuments the later megalithic structure encapsulates an earlier timber and earthen long barrow. What we see today is in essence a restoration of the later monument following the archaeological excavations undertaken by Stuart Piggott and Richard Atkinson in the early 1960's. An interesting feature of the stone work is the use of smaller stones between the megalithic uprights of the facade and interior chambers, effectively dry stone walling, the like of which you would associate with the Cotswolds. There's a very good reason for this. The style of construction and layout of the ground plan is to all intents and purposes of the class known to archaeologists as the Cotswold-Severn Group. West Kennett long barrow is of the same type and reflects the influences that most certainly extended into this area of the country from further north and west. When this site was in use as a mortuary house, house of the dead, call it what you will, the Ridgeway passed by nearer than it does now, within 25-30mts. This ancient track not only allowed for the passage of people, livestock and trade, but was a corridor for ideas and beliefs, culture if you like.

Associated with Wayland's Smithy is the tale of Wayland the smith, a demigod of Saxon mythology, after whom the monument has been named. Basically legend says it's Wayland who is supposed to have made the shoes for the White Horse of Uffington and that if your horse has shed a shoe and you leave it tethered, along with a silver coin on the roof of the 'cave', then upon your return you'll find the horse re-shod and the money gone, payment for Wayland's work. The use of the word cave can be taken to mean the appearance of the burial chambers, which like those at West Kennett do resemble the interior of a cave. In the Saxon period when this monument acquired its name, the chambers would probably have still been partially blocked off by the closing facade of megaliths. Over time some of the facade stones will have fallen whilst others were no doubt dislodged by tomb robbers, most likely the Saxons if the Romans hadn't already beaten them to it. Later antiquarian and archaeological excavations left the monument open to the elements. Prior to the 1960's, only one of the burial chambers still retained its covering capstone. It was in this semi derelict state, when my mother was first introduced to the site as a child.

Like so many people before, my mother was told the story of Wayland and like so many people since, came away that little richer for the experience. By this I mean she not only took in the atmosphere and antiquity of the place but took away with her the odd coin or two, for like the need of so many people to throw a coin in a fountain many feel the need to go along with the legend, well at least in part! In my own childhood I remember locating the odd coin pushed into a crevice or left boldly for all to see on the surface of a stone. Mind you, values must have slipped, as I don't remember ever coming across a silver coin, copper only. I must admit to having left coins here myself as an adult and at similar sites around the country over the years. Quite why we do it I don't rightly know, but I suppose it simply helps to unite us with our ancestors. I expect the local Moonraker's perpetuated the myth in order to help supplement their incomes! We are now in Oxfordshire, not Wiltshire, having crossed the county boundary just over a mile west of here, but this was always a grey area! Mind you prior to the county boundary changes, that took place on April 1st 1974, Berkshire had laid claim to Wayland's Smithy and its unique neighbour the White Horse of Uffington upon its hill. Who was the fool then, I ask myself, who allowed such changes to take place?

Over the years I have introduced many friends, family and loved ones to Wayland's Smithy. In order to see and feel the changing moods of the place, I have stayed overnight on three separate occasions. Each time I shared the experience with others but failed to convince them that the burial chambers would be a really snug place to sleep! Twice I've slept under canvas next to the tomb, but the first stopover was spent without a tent, huddled in a sleeping bag on a groundsheet, my head shoved in my rucksack against the cold. My friend lay a few feet away, parallel to me. Oh I forgot to say, we had bedded down in the ruts of the Ridgeway itself. On that occasion my mate wasn't prepared to sleep anywhere near the tomb and our early morning wakeup call was heralded by the put-put-put of a Massey-Ferguson tractor drawing near. The following year, however, the same mate was part of a party I led on a walk along the Ridgeway from Foxhill to Streatley when we camped alongside the tomb. The location is truly atmospheric at sunset on a crisp winter's day, heaven on a warm autumn day and just magic at dawn on a hot summer's day.

Quite why this Neolithic tomb was constructed where it is remains a mystery. What drove the builders to place it here? It's interesting that the entrance faces south-southeast, not over the vastness of the vale below. My own belief is that the entrance looked out over the ancestral farmlands, the rolling Downs, and that like many of the houses of the living, faced the morning sun. Death I believe, for our distant ancestors at least, was just another stage on a journey to immortality. From the evidence found, here and at other similar sites, fires and feasting along with ritual cleansing and ordering of the bones seems to hint at ancestor worship and communal gatherings other than at the time of burial. Added to the above is what might be seen as a strange piece of evidence, the incorporation of several saddle querns used in the construction of the earlier earthen long barrow. Saddle querns are basically large pieces of stone measuring on average 75cm to a metre long by 50cm wide and 40cm deep. Their purpose was for use in grinding grain into flour and they were in general use up to, and including, the Iron Age, at which time the rotary hand quern tended to supersede them. The miller knelt with the saddle stone between their knees and introduced grain onto the top surface, then a separate rounded stone was held in both hands and used as a crusher/grinder. This action over time resulted in a concave recess being formed in the upper surface of the stone giving the appearance of a horses' saddle, thus the prefix saddle being applied by archaeologists. Found in this context, I can think of at least two theories to explain their presence over and above just simple reuse because they happened to be available. Bread and other foods utilising bruised or ground grain and incorporating wild seeds, nuts and weeds etc. would have formed a high proportion of the staple diet. The saddle quern represents the tool that processed the food of life. This in turn leads on to a desire for good harvests and fertility of the land. Saddle querns therefore in this context may well be votive offerings to appease the gods, but equally they may be seen as symbols of the high esteem in society that the deceased held as providers of the daily bread.

Finally, before leaving this special place enclosed within its setting of beech trees, it's worth pointing out that the view we see today from here of The White Horse on its hill and Uffington Castle, the latter's banks and ditches silhouetted on the skyline, is very different from what the makers of this monument would have seen. Back then, neither of these antiquities existed. They were to come into being at least three thousand years later, a longer period of time than that which now divides us from them!

12. Whitehorse Hill.

Whitehorse Hill at 248m (856ft) dominates The Vale of White Horse. When seen on a good day from out in the vale if travelling on the Reading to Swindon railway line, the White Horse appears to be galloping up and across the hill, it's strangely shaped beaked head looking more like a dragon than a horse. From this vantage point the undulating outline of the Iron Age period fort that sits astride the crest of the hill is also clearly seen. When the light is right, early or late in the year often is best, shadows cast by the setting sun throws the entire hill into relief. Particularly striking is The Manger, the steep sided dry valley that fronts the hill. Even if the White Horse were not part of the scene this is without doubt a beautiful hill, acting as it does as a backcloth to the vale below.

I've already alluded to the tale of the supposed cutting of the horse as a celebration by Alfred on his victory over the Danes at the battle of Ashdown in 871AD. That story aside, there are few firm facts about the origins of this most famous of chalk cut horse hill figures. The figure plays an important part in local folk tradition, principally via the writings of Thomas Hughes, author of 'Tom Brown's Schooldays', who lived in Uffington and who also wrote 'Scouring of the White Horse' in 1857. This 'scouring' of the horse to remove grass and to retain its shape is well documented and although said to have been carried out at regular intervals of seven years, this appears to be far from the truth, with sporadic scouring being often as not the norm. Overzealous scouring may well have led to the shape of the horse changing a little. Much has been made of this possibility, resulting in an assortment of 'original' designs being postulated from sleek thoroughbreds and carthorses through to barrel shaped ponies reminiscent of Thelwell's with a leg at each corner! Whatever changes have taken place to its outline over the years, I feel certain that it has not varied so very much from what we see today. I say this from comparing it to more recent figures that have overall retained their original outline, significant change being seldom seen. No, I'm sure that in the minds of the local populace who undertook to maintain the figure, the emphasis was on retaining the integrity of the form as a matter of some pride. Scouring was accompanied with fun and games, often a fair and market, a time for getting together and thoroughly enjoying the occasion. One particular game involved a cartwheel being rolled down the hillside into The Manger and adult males of the district giving chase. The one who managed to catch the wheel, or got nearest to it, won a cheese as his prize.

From the design of the horse we can see there is a direct correlation with Iron Age coinage, the so-called 'Celtic' coinage of ancient Britain that was in circulation at the time of Caesar's forays in 55 and again in 54BC. This stylised horse form appears on gold coins known as staters, and on the lesser silver and bronze units issued by various tribal groups throughout the south of Britain and indeed Gaul, present day France. Often depicted along with a spoked wheel, they are degenerate copies of coins originally produced for Philip 11 of Macedonia, father of Alexander the great, in the mid fourth century BC depicting a chariot and horses. Do we see here a direct link in the chariot wheel on the coins and the cartwheel from the game above? This link with the Greek world prior to its conquest by Rome reflects a common ancestry and culture, one in which the esteem in which the horse was held played an important part in the beliefs of the day.

Such importance was attached to the horse that it was deemed as a deity by our forefathers, Epona, the horse goddess. As such, it's not such a big leap to identify with the commonly held belief that the White Horse of Uffington is indeed a representation of Epona and most likely was a totem used by the ruling tribe in the area who would no doubt have constructed and occupied the hill fort above. That tribe was the Atrebates, although some authorities, including English Heritage, would say the Dobunni, rulers of what was the better part of Berkshire along with parts of Wiltshire, Oxfordshire and Hampshire. Is it any wonder then that such a furore was made when in 1974 the county boundary changes brought Whitehorse Hill within the auspices of Oxfordshire, thereby relinquishing the sacred site to the enemy? By enemy I mean the former tribal people called the Catuvllauni who had held sway over much of present day Oxfordshire and the Thames basin. In the early 1990's archaeological excavations along with ground breaking scientific dating analysis was able to point to the period in which the horse was cut into the hill. These activities confirmed its prehistoric date, there being the added possibility that it was made as early as the late Bronze Age. If the dating is to be relied upon, then the horse might be contemporary with the prototypes of the coinage that circulated in the Greek world during Alexander the Great's lifetime.

As to how the act of wishing on the horses eye came about I'm not sure but can only surmise it relates to asking for the god's favour, much the same as making a wish at a well or spring. The only real difference, here being that originally your wish was paid for by your subservience in taking part in the scouring. A similar tradition is to be seen associated with the Cerne Abbas Giant in Dorset, a huge chalk hill figure of a male deity sporting an erect phallus. The giant has taken on the mantle of a fertility god, Hercules in particular. According to 18th century writings, wishes centred on the procurement of children by newlyweds and barren wives, couples sometimes spending the night between the giant's thighs! But as opposed to the undoubted antiquity of Uffington White Horse, it being noted in documents from as early as the eleventh century, the Cerne giant is only documented from the eighteenth century. This suggests the figure is only three hundred years old, or thereabouts, as such an important feature in the landscape would not have gone unreported. This then just goes to show how a folk tradition and mythology can be built around a so-called 'antiquity' in a comparatively short period of time. Bearing the above in mind, folk tales and other mythology must be looked at with caution.

Nestling below the sinuous lines of the White Horse, and divided from it by the road that takes you to the top of the hill, is the conical flat-topped mound known as Dragon Hill. This perches on the side of its larger neighbour and overlooks The Manger. The mound is for the best part grassed around its circumference, but the flat top exhibits bare areas where it is said the grass never grows. This last snippet of information ties in with the legend attached to the hill that it was here that St. George slew the dragon, hence its name and the comparatively bare top, the bare areas being where the dragon's blood was spilt. To all intents and purposes the mound appears to be a natural appendage of the main hill, although man might well have levelled the summit at some time in the past. Such levelling would fit in well with the needs of anyone overseeing the scouring of the horse, the site providing a level viewpoint for directing operations and acting as a refreshment area. Unfortunately archaeological excavations carried out on the site in the 1990's have added little to our understanding of its use and relationship, if any, to the horse, having said that, an earlier soil sample taken from the summit revealed double the concentration of potash that is found normally in the surrounding area. This infers that wood has been burnt on the site over time. Perhaps we have evidence here for the merrymaking associated with the scouring of the horse; you know the sort of thing, a bonfire for cooking your sausages on! Other possibilities perhaps are that this was the site for a beacon or a stopping place for early tourist ascending the hill on mules? Whatever use the mound has been put to over the years, I'm sure that it has given pleasure to all who have climbed it as it stands in a most dramatic spot.

The Manger falls away below Whitehorse Hill looking green and verdant. Its name is assumed to relate to the White Horse, it being an oversized feed container for the mare above! Perhaps though we should be looking at this another way, the richness of the grass providing grazing for a whole herd of horses, horses that might well have pulled the chariots of the elite in the fortress above? Another option is that the name comes from the Saxon 'mangere' monger as in fishmonger, in other words a trader. This latter option ties in well with the practise of holding a fair or market on the site at the time of the scouring.

Staying with the horse theme for the moment, I am reminded of the one and only time I had direct contact with the hunt, the foxhunt that is. It was a glorious sunny summer's day when I was walking with a friend exploring Whitehorse Hill. We had just ascended the lower slope of the hill on a path that comes out on the road on the uphill side of Dragon Hill above The Manger. It was just as we approached the gate from the field onto the road that we became aware of a lone rider on a large horse traversing the hill and making for the same gate. We arrived at the gate at the same time where upon the rider looked down at me from on high. No words being spoken I however knew instinctively that I was required to open the gate for the horse and rider to pass through. The gate negotiated, the rider made off over the road and up the opposite slope of the hill with a feint gesture of a thank you by a wave of the hand. I closed the gate behind us as my friend gave me a quizzing look. I knew what he was thinking, 'Why open the gate for a toff? You might as well have tugged your forelock at the same time'. Well, I was an impressionable seventeen-year-old and easily intimidated, especially by a huge horse towering over me. But the truth be known, the rider was a mature good-looking women in her thirties I'd say and I was bowled over by the encounter. Ah but then I've always had a thing for the older woman!

Further up the hill we heard the hunt and then a few minutes later saw the spectacle as horses and hounds in full chase followed the fox. And what a spectacle it was. Even at the distance we were from the action, the noise along with the colour, smell and vibration beneath our feet sent a shiver down my spine. This was perhaps the nearest I would come to the sights, sounds and smells, along with the fear, that an ordinary peasant foot soldier would have experienced when facing a cavalry charge. The sound of the hound master's horn brought me back to reality and I watched in silence as the fox made it to the edge of the wood bordering the Kingston Lisle road. Hounds now ran in all directions as the riders converged on the wood. For several minutes all was confusion before the hounds were called off and the hunt continued up and over the hill. I guess that on that occasion the fox gave them the slip.

Above the White Horse, and before the fort is reached, is the slight remains of a long mound. This mound along with others barely visible in the vicinity is of Neolithic and Bronze Age origin. Excavations in the long mound back in 1857 by Martin-Atkins, the Lord of the Manor, revealed the remains of some 36 individuals believed to date from the late Roman period. These remains consisted of 19 adult males, 16 women and a young lad. Dating was based on the finding of bronze coins in the mouths of some of the bodies, a custom associated with paying Chiron, the ferryman, to take the deceased across the river Styx in the underworld. Nearby was said to be a smaller mound containing 6 more individuals along with a further assortment of bones. Two of the bodies had been decapitated. The dating has been confirmed as late Roman by the 1990's excavations. Quite what this tells us is a little confusing, but the probable scenario is that the larger group represents the local Romano-British population inhabiting the fort, whilst the smaller group is more likely to be criminals who were disposed of with little ceremony, decapitation being carried out after death to prevent the spirit walking.

When taken into consideration with the few facts that have come to light, again following on after the 1990's excavations, the above might represent a skirmish as originally postulated by Martin-Atkins. This may well have happened during a period of civil unrest towards, or shortly after, the collapse of Roman rule in Britain. Findings within the fort suggest that the Iron Age fortifications were pressed back into use during the late Roman occupation and possibly in the Saxon period too. Evidence is slim, but some sort of temporary occupation of the site in the Roman period is indicated with breeches being made in the walls and occupational debris being found. Together with the reuse of the earlier burial mounds as a cemetery outside the walls, all this points towards a change in the social conditions one would expect to find at this time.

The fort as we see it now is rather less impressive than either Barbury or Liddington and was likely never to have been of the same stature. That being said the location merits taking time to drink in the view. Even on the busiest Bank holiday, you can escape from the worse of the crowds and have a little of the downland turf to yourself if you're prepared to walk to the further boundary. Here you can lay in the grass and gaze up at the blue, blue sky, whilst a lark hovering overhead will as likely serenade you. This is one of the most pleasant of memories I share with my wife. Alternatively you can join the throng on the lip of the hill and watch the kites being flown, the occasional paraglider or if you're really lucky, a kestrel hunting for its lunch! One experience I would choose not to repeat is being foolish enough to push my mother in her wheelchair up the so-called disabled access route to the viewpoint above the White Horse. This was undertaken one hot summer's day when I was some years younger, but the strain nearly did for me! My mother enjoyed the opportunity to take in the view little knowing that for her it was to be for the last time.

13. Of drought, police and wild camping.

To the south and east of The Ridgeway the downs run back from the northwest facing escarpment in rounded folds divided by narrow valleys for the most part. Located within these valleys are small settlements where water is to be found. Other than at a few points where the ridge drops to lower ground there is virtually no habitation on the ridge proper other than a few isolated farms that rely on artesian wells for their water, or water being pumped from further afield. This lack of water makes for thirsty travellers on foot in drought conditions. Such conditions are not so uncommon over short periods of time, but can become prolonged, as was the case in 1975. It was in August that year that I walked The Ridgeway, along with my future wife at the time, from Streatley to Swindon.

Having set out from Streatley late in the day, the first inkling that all was not well was once we had ascended the downs and stopped en route to cool down at a cattle trough. Normally fresh water could be obtained for washing and for drinking if boiled, but this was dry. Further along the track we came across another trough with a water cistern above. Again the same story, but here some water remained in the bottom of the cistern below the level of the outflow. Although fairly stale, we however used the water to cool ourselves by wetting our sunhats, tee shirts etcetera. What little water we had with us we felt obliged to ration under the circumstances as it became apparent that no fresh drinking water was to be had. After some 7 miles the heat began to take its toll, we accordingly looked for a suitable campsite. The crossing of the A34 at Gore Hill offered what appeared to be a likely spot alongside the track. The last of the fresh water finished and only some Coke left, a decision was made that I walk down into East Ilsey to get more provisions. A mile and a half later I found myself in the only place open where any form of food and drink was to be had a roadside pub! Even then, the little they had to offer left a lot to be desired. I returned after first downing a quick pint. Back at camp my future wife had partially pitched the tent in order to gain some shade. We sat down that evening to a repast of warmed up stew along with a mixture of crisps, chocolate and a jar of cockles, the only food I could procure from the pub! As for water, that had come in the form of bottled beer and more coke.

Settling down that night we soon fell asleep exhausted from the exertions of the day. But our peace and quiet was later to be shattered by what was to be one of the weirdest happenings I have experienced. Around midnight we were awakened by the noise of a car coming to a stand not so very far from the front of the tent, its headlights full on looking like two glaring eyes filtered through the nylon. We lay half-awake straining to make out what was happening outside, feeling very vulnerable in our little cocooned world. It's amazing how your mind can go off on flights of fancy when faced with a situation such as this. Were we about to be attacked by modern-day highwaymen? Was a pair of crazed escaped prisoners on the loose? Were these local youths out joy riding in a stolen car? All these thoughts and more flashed through our brains. The beam from a torch was to be seen coming towards the tent along with the sounds from heavy footfalls. We shrank back under the sleeping bag not daring to make a sound. Then, to our amazement came a tap,

tap, tap made by the knuckles of someone's hand on the aluminium upright followed by a deep throaty voice, "Police. We wish to know who's in there and where you've come from". On hearing this we both sighed with relief, if not a little embarrassment too. I slipped some trousers on and fumbled with the zip on the tent flaps at the same time as answering the questions. Having gingerly stuck my head out two policemen confronted me, one towering over me and the other crouching at face level shining his torch into my eyes. I held open the flap and the officer shined his torch into the tent at which my companion raised her head whilst covering her modesty with the sleeping bag. Turning back to me the officer then ordered me to show him my knuckles. Perplexed I did as I was told. This seemed to satisfy him and he withdrew allowing me to rise to my feet. What transpired was that a fellow male police officer had been severely beaten-up in nearby Newbury and the search had gone out for the culprits. It was only later after the police had left that we laughed, a nervous laugh, about the thought of me being suspected of beating a police officer to a pulp with my bare fists. I stand just 5'5'' tall and at the time weighed somewhere in the region of just eight stone.

The next morning we ate the remainder of the stew and drank Coke for breakfast, we couldn't face the cockles! Striking camp early we continued on our way. The plan was to make for Whitehorse Hill and hopefully secure fresh water from one of the only two farms astride the Ridgeway five miles further on. By Ridgeway Down the lack of water was again becoming a problem as the sun now beamed down from a cloudless sky. Beneath the monument that commemorates Lord Wantage we drank the last of our Coke, a mile short of the nearest farm. Pressing on, our spirits dropped upon reaching Whitehouse Farm as outside was a handwritten notice stating "No Water", obviously we were not the first to have passed that way. The same was the case at Angeldown Farm. By now water was our overall consideration. At Segsbury Camp, Letcombe Castle as it's known by some people, we decided to drop off the ridge and try our luck in the villages below. Passing swiftly through the fort, which I'll come back to later, we walked the mile or so into Letcombe Regis.

Now well below the spring line and with access to mains water, our luck was in. Although water was being rationed the local pub was very helpful. A good meal and a hearty drink left us feeling refortified. Between here and its sister village of Letcombe Bassett we were able to restock both our food and water supplies. We now felt sufficiently revived to admire the watercress beds and the village churches, not to mention the local vernacular of the houses! Our walk continued that day up Gramp's Hill back onto The Ridgeway and via Whitehorse Hill before camping for the night at possibly my favourite location hereabouts yes you've guessed it, Wayland's Smithy. By the way, it should be said that casual wild-camping in those days was not a problem. Nowadays I'd recommend permission be sought before bedding down for the night.

14. The back of beyond.

Up to now, other than a brief diversion or two, I have kept basically to The Ridgeway proper. But as stated earlier, ridges with intervening valleys, or coombs, run at right angles to the main escarpment providing a happy hunting ground for antiquities and other things. It is to this 'back of beyond' that I now wish to draw your attention.

Perhaps of greatest leisure interest to many are the training gallops that can be seen right across the region. Unfortunately I suspect that for a high proportion of these people, they seldom get the benefit to be had of walking the downs over which their favourite fillies workout. The epicentre of horse training in this part of the world is Lambourn. Around the mid 1930's my mother went to be a live-in house servant in one of the large houses in the area. She was around fifteen and the first time away from home, home being a simple two up two down red brick terraced house in Swindon lived in by her parents and younger brother, not a big family by the standards of the day. Well her new plush surroundings and new job was short lived, something to do with her spilling polish over a stone hearth and staining it whilst attempting to polish the grate. She was asked to leave. So ended what might have proved a life in servitude, in a beautiful part of the county it has to be said!

Situated some two miles to the north of Lambourn alongside the minor road from Kingston Lisle is the pre-historic cemetery known as Lambourn Seven Barrows. Dating from the Bronze Age the site sits below the southern end of Pit Down that affords easy access to The Ridgeway path. This concentration of barrows, numbering in reality well over twenty, exhibits the range of barrow types to be found hereabouts. Round, bell, disc and pond along with an outlying long barrow, the latter of earlier Neolithic vintage, provide an ideal assemblage in one location for anyone interested in looking at the classified forms of ancient burial monuments. Lambourn Seven Barrows is a Scheduled Ancient Monument cared for by English Heritage, formerly the Department of the Environment, DOE. When visiting the site look out for the early cast iron notice warning you not to cause any damage to the site, a piece of history and an antiquity in its own right. The scheduled area affords not only protection to the cemetery from ploughing, excavation and the like, but in so doing provides a perfect habitat for the naturally occurring wild flowers to be found in a chalk downland environment. During a visit in July 1997 the site was a riot of colour, the flowers in full bloom and acting as hosts to a myriad of butterflies. Heaven, sheer heaven!

It was during the above visit upon returning to our car that my future wife and I were accosted by a local who walked up to us, and beaming all over his face, demanded to know how long we had been married. Quite why he should have asked this very pointed question left us amused to say the least. The man appeared to be in his fifties and was wearing an old worn suit with a collar and tie in the heat of the day. We came to the conclusion that he was a penny short of a shilling, probably the result of very local interbreeding, a true 'village idiot' meant in the kindest of ways. Anyway, he was a very cheerful chap who obviously thought that if you held hands with your partner, even more, kissed, you just had to be married! As it happens we had known each other just two weeks.

Some four miles to the northwest of Lambourn is Ashdown House, a fine mid. 17th century Dutch-style house set within its own parkland. Purchased by the National Trust in 1956 this is a property I have failed to visit, catching only the odd glimpse of high chimneystacks and hipped roof surmounted by its ogee cupola through the trees. Whilst the house itself is obviously of immense interest for its architecture along with its associations with Elizabeth of Bohemia (The Winter Queen), sister of Charles 1st. there are clues to an earlier house on the site. The parkland to the south of the house is surrounded by the remains of a 'pale', a bank and ditch that would originally have been surmounted by a wooden palisade or more likely a thorn hedge, normally associated with mediaeval deer parks; whilst to the west, bordering the park is the site of Alfred's Castle. Alfred's Castle is a neat circular earthwork of Iron Age date but having strong local traditions with being the fortification used by Alfred prior to his defeat of the Danes at the battle of Ashdown. That being as it may, the site presents a compact fortified settlement, much smaller than say Liddington or Barbury, but presumably forming part of the chain of forts that secured The Ridgeway along with its commerce.

Within a couple of miles to the southwest are several Romano-British, Iron Age and earlier settlement sites. The concentration of multi-period sites points to the continuity of farming within the area, with arable as well as stock rearing. Some of these sites have been known since the Victorian period, a result of ploughing and other agricultural practices bringing artefacts and building debris to the surface. In the late 1960's and early 1970's further discoveries were made by SAARG as a direct result of emergency archaeological excavations necessitated by the building of the M4 motorway. During that campaign our efforts were somewhat haphazard, much depending on the goodwill of the developers and the availability of volunteers to work at short notice, mainly at weekends. Being small of stature I often found myself allocated a refuse or grain storage pit to excavate, or the occasional cesspit! The former often contain the latter making for rich pickings so to speak. Grain storage pits were in everyday use in the pre-Roman period and comprised of a large hole up to two meters deep by one or two in diameter cut into the solid chalk of the downs. Once the pit was lined with straw and filled with grain the top would be closed off with a wicker cover or similar and possibly sealed with clay. This normally resulted in the contents heating up, the straw actually carbonising and thereby forming a further protective barrier from degradation by moisture, rodents and water percolation. Where the above process went wrong it would often as not produce a soggy decomposed mess, the silo then being pressed into use as another refuse pit. The contents of such pits, comprising for the best part animal bone, broken pots and stone tools, charcoal, carbonised cereal grain and the like, prove to be veritable resources for research into the everyday lives of our ancestors. From the above meagre finds can be seen what types of grain was grown and livestock raised and eaten, what local materials was sourced and used in the manufacture of tools, utensils and buildings. We can also date the deposits from the style and type of pottery and tools found, thereby working out a chronology for the sites.

Of course, where the M4 Motorway has been driven through the downs, no sign of the settlements and agricultural activities associated with them is to be seen, witness the landscaping at Badbury Wick Roman villa. All has been obliterated or covered over, but much crucial information was retrieved along with site plans and some artefacts. Since those days however, science and technological advances have moved on and now things would be very different. Anyone who has watched the television 'Time Team' series will have an understanding of just what is possible, much of which can be done in a non-intrusive fashion. But resources then were very limited, especially financial funding. This often led to finds being boxed up and stored away out of sight in the bowels of our museums, or often as not in the loft or garden shed belonging to devoted amateur archaeologists. Reports on the findings were slow in appearing, if at all, and there was little accountability. Now if such work is carried out, as for example the upgrading of the A30 through Devon in the late 1990's, the 'developer' has to pay for archaeological research, excavation and post-excavation reports and museum storage space along with the conservation of any artefacts found. This has come about mainly through the implementation of government planning legislation in the form of Planning Policy Guidelines, PPG's (now updated yet again). Whilst at first glance this regime appears to be the answer to all our dreams, many feel that it does a disservice in that pure research excavations are fewer, 'developers', especially homeowners wishing to develop their property, are often put off by the extra expense incurred and the role of the keen amateur is felt to be under threat from bureaucracy. Such is the present state in the world of archaeology and for better or for worse this is the system we now have to operate under.

Many good things however came out of the M4 archaeological excavations, notably the experience gained by so many amateur archaeologists, which led to some of us pursuing archaeology and the interpretation of our heritage as a career. Two of the leading lights in SAARG went on to rediscover the remains of the Roman villa in the grounds of Littlecote House near to Chilton Foliat. The site lies alongside the Roman road from Cunetio, Mildenhall, to Calleva, Silchester. This led to a program of excavation and conservation covering some thirteen years, from 1978 to 1991. The owners of the site paid for funding to a great degree, originally Sir Seton Wills followed by Peter de Savary. The latter was owner at the time of other heritage sites including Land's End and John o' Groats! Littlecote may be seen to be straying from the point of this collection of tales, it being quite some distance from The Ridgeway proper. But in my defense for its inclusion, and what you must keep in mind, is the social and political set-up that existed in the Roman period in that the owner of such an important villa as this would in all probability have also owned the assortment of smaller Romanised settlements and buildings that cover the area. In effect we're looking at a country estate with the villa at its centre.

Littlecote illustrates well the layout and opulence that a leading villa of the day boasted. Not only were there the usual domestic and servants quarters, kitchens and associated store rooms, stables etcetera, but also bath suits, banqueting halls and guests rooms with mosaic floors and hypocausts, the latter being under-floor heating. The floors depicted images of gods and scenes from Roman mythology such as the exquisite Orpheus mosaic, a far cry from the large crude tesserae recovered from the site of the ploughed-out Roman building on Russley Downs. Here by contrast, we have what appears to be a local Romano-British landowner trying his best to emulate his Roman superiors within his limited means. Tesserae by the way are the cubes of stone, baked clay, glass and other materials that have been cut to size by hand in order to facilitate the range of colours and detail required in achieving the intricacy to be seen in many of the better quality mosaic floors. The rooms from which these tesserae came however would in all probability have been unheated, apart from free standing braziers and lack any fine detailing, the tesserae cubes being large and forming part of a simple tesselated geometric design. Whilst on the subject of mosaics, Roman literature relates that it was not uncommon for a child, who had transgressed in some way, to be punished by being made to stand barefoot in a room heated by a hypocaust. The inference here is that a slave was made to fire up the furnace that fed the under-floor heating system to such ferocity that it made standing barefoot on the surface of the mosaic near on intolerable!

The Roman villa at Littlecote might in some ways be seen to overshadow the importance of the later post-mediaeval country house on the site. Littlecote though is a fine example of an Elizabethan house of the highest quality standing as it does in grounds laid out to the later designs of Capability Brown. Encapsulated within the house are the remnants of an earlier mediaeval one with 17th and 18th century, Victorian and Edwardian additions sympathetically blended. Pevsner in his 'Buildings of Wiltshire' waxes lyrical about the house, which is high praise indeed. Of greater significance than the architecture for military historians is the superb collection of English Civil War period arms and armour that is housed here. Muskets, swords, pistols, breastplates, helmets and numerous other artefacts are to be seen; but what makes the greatest impression for me are the quality and the number of buff coats on display. Such a show of this calibre is rarely seen, let alone in a private collection. All of the above was viewed some years ago. Then, guides giving the tour of the house told the story of the events surrounding the murder of a newborn child and of how the ghost of the baby's mother is said to walk the corridors lamenting her loss, all chilling stuff. Now the house is a hotel, so public access and ownership of the collection may well be different.

This then should give you a flavour of the gems to be discovered in and around 'the back of beyond'. But perhaps of equal importance is simply the majesty of the open countryside with its miles of rough farm tracks, bridal ways and footpaths. Walk 'the back of beyond' and you enter another world. This is horse rearing and grain growing country where the fields are big to match the sky, where in places bright red poppies grow thick amongst the golden wheat creating a scene and an atmosphere that would not be out of place in a Monet picture. This is also an area where you are just as likely to come across something a little out of the ordinary. Walking one such track hereabouts I encountered a family approaching me from the opposite direction with what appeared at a distance to be a very large white 'dog' on a leash. As I drew closer the 'dog' turned out to be a goat, its horns capped with orange tennis balls!

15. Segsbury Camp & The Ridgeway forts.

As previously mentioned, Segsbury is also known as Letcombe Regis Castle after the twin villages in the vale below. Segsbury stands to the north of The Ridgeway right on the lip of the escarpment and dominates the approaches to the downs from what would have been the nearest crossing of the Thames around Abingdon. Wantage, birthplace of King Alfred, lies just over a couple of miles to the north. Due however to the farming regime in the vicinity, mainly cereal crops as opposed to open grazing for sheep, the fort has a strangely different feel to that of its western counterparts. When approached from The Ridgeway along the track that passes through the fort and on down into the vale, you can be forgiven for thinking that here we have a lesser fort, one that is inferior in size, structure, call it what you wish. The ramparts just don't seem to tower above you in the same way as those at Barbury or Uffington. In reality they are every bit as impressive, but because over much of their circumference they are covered in scrub and trees and the interior, along with the exterior, is used for cultivation, the banks seem to shrink into the flora. That said I have only visited Segsbury during the height of the summer when the crops were at their tallest.

The fort encloses some 26 acres, by far the largest area taken in by any of the forts along our stretch of The Ridgeway and quite a respectable area when compared to the 8½ acres of Uffington. During my visits back in the 1970's and 80's it was possible to walk round the top of the defences provided that you were prepared to push yourself through the scrub and bushes after first gaining access via an overgrown stile in the fence. Look carefully and you'll see the odd sarcen protruding through the grass and undergrowth, remnants of the stone that once faced the banks of the fort. When conditions are right, the interior of the fort is like a sea of grass, the crop swaying in the breeze.

The size of the fort calls for some questions. Why is the interior area of Segsbury so much larger than the other forts? Do we have here the most important location in the area during the Iron Age? Was it a tribal capital? These two questions are not only difficult to answer, but most likely impossible to answer. In many cases the area and to a certain extent the ground plan of hill forts was governed by the topography of the ground. This can clearly be seen in forts such as Clay Hill here in Wiltshire and Maiden Castle, Dorset. The former is perched on the top of an isolated hill leaving little room for expansion, indeed the banks and ditches utilise the steep contour of the hill partly in an effort to take in as much ground as is possible. In the case of Maiden Castle the earliest fort on the site used approximately only a third of the available space on the top of the hill before being extended some one hundred years later so as to encompass the entire hill. Many other examples could be quoted of hill forts taking in the entire ground available. In a lot of cases there is evidence of earlier use made of sites for instance bronze- age barrows within the earthworks of Cley Hill, whilst at Maiden Castle can be seen an earthen burial barrow some 1,800ft long, also the ghost of a Neolithic causewayed camp dating to around 3,500bc. Causewayed camps by the way, such as the fine example at Windmill Hill not far from Avebury, do not appear to have been built for defence against enemies due to the low banks and numerous entrances accessed by causeways giving this type of monument their name. Other factors, such as large amounts of rubbish found in the ditches, point towards these monuments being used primarily as focal points for cattle management, gatherings and feasting. Such was the nature of many so called 'forts' according to some archaeologists, but in the cases of those described here on The Ridgeway I would venture another theory.

Our Ridgeway 'forts' all appear to be of a single phase in construction, apart that is from Ram's Hill a mile or so to the east of Uffington Castle. This 'fort' unusually lies just a few yards to the south of The Ridgeway. I've not mentioned Ram's hill before as there is only vestiges of it to be seen, much having been ploughed away or eroded by the weather. What we have here is an earlier earthwork from the Bronze Age that had fallen out of use and the site subsequently reused in the Iron Age with later changes made in the Roman period. Evidence for this dating comes from excavations carried out in 1939, again by the late Professor Stuart Piggott. The opinion is that the earlier earthworks are considered to be an 'enclosure', the Iron Age phase a hill-fort and the Roman additions a settlement. The term 'enclosure' here really means an area enclosed by a modest ditch and bank probably surmounted by a thicket hedge or fence, not obviously of a defensive nature. Such sites are normally seen as stock paddocks or corrals. But as with many early landscape features you have to be careful in allocating a definitive use without good evidence. An example of this is the 'pale' in Ashdown Park already spoken of. Whilst to all intents and purposes this landscape feature resembles the present feature under discussion, we know from historical sources that the 'pale' was constructed in the 13th century for the Abbot of Glastonbury. In this case David Disbury, from whom the reference has been got in his guide 'On and around Whitehorse Hill' goes on to say the 'pale' was constructed in order "to protect his woods from wondering animals". This then is a totally different use from that envisaged at Ram's Hill or associated with other 'enclosures'.

Moving on to the 'hill-fort', the general term given to what is commonly held to be the function of the numerous Iron Age sites already looked at. As we have seen, those on our stretch of The Ridgeway tend to exhibit features associated with defence in depth; that being multiple banks and ditches, elevated positions giving good wide views and sites that not only dominate the line of The Ridgeway but also that of the surrounding area; or do they? Whilst multiple defences are in evidence at Barbury, most lack this kind of defence on the more easily attacked elevations facing onto the level approaches where you would expect to find them. Most of the forts feature just two or even one original entrance making for ease of defence requiring fewer defenders at what is the natural weak point. Within the enclosed area is plenty of space suitable for huts, animals and troops. Where our forts display a common theme is in the apparent use of virgin sites, at least not exhibiting earlier use than the Iron Age in any substantial way. In fact it's this sudden development of numerous large defended positions along the line of The Ridgeway that goes towards adding weight to the idea that they form part of an overall military plan in defending and controlling passage along this important prehistoric artery. This implies a single controlling power, a confederation of local families making up a tribal unit or, small independent power bases each competing for a bite of the cherry in exacting payment for safe passage. The latter is less likely to be the case, but might go some way in explaining the varied size of the forts. Size reflects not only the area required to house men and stable animals but possibly the status and prestige of the tribe or overlord. What must not be overlooked when taking this question of size into the equation is that the locations in which all these forts have been built are not constricted, size therefore was determined by factors other than the topography. No, I believe these forts represent centres of power that could hold large numbers of cattle, harvested crops and men to guard them if needs be.

What the above tells me is that the Iron Age period in this area was one of plenty. Beef on the hoof along with cereal crops were the mainstay of the economy. Wealth was counted in such basic commodities and who controlled that wealth, was a lord indeed. Add to this the traffic in high status luxury goods that we have seen passed along The Ridgeway in the possession of traders, emissaries from tribal alliances and travelling craftsmen, bringing with them the latest fashions and news from far and wide. Here we have a society in which there was surplus foodstuffs to provide the necessary subsidence for the huge labour force required to construct such large municipal works as hill forts. Our hill forts then should be seen as collective gathering places for people, yes defensible when and if required against the odd marauding band, but primarily huge holding areas with the power and prestige of the tribe or lord symbolically emphasised by the size and location of the forts. This was a period when the arts and craft skills flourished, when show and outward display in the form of decorated jewellery, clothing and weaponry went over the top to impress. It's only towards the end of the Roman period that we begin to see actual evidence of military use of the hill forts in this area and then, by what appears to be the civilian population undertaking punitive measures at defending itself against insurgents, mercenaries running amok and invaders. Unlike the more western and southern hill forts such as Maiden Castle and Hod Hill in Dorset for example, where Roman activity can be seen integral to the early years of invasion and occupation, our forts do not exhibit any similar evidence. There are no Roman forts built within the hill forts, no evidence of having been taken by force and no sign of signal stations used in relaying messages at speed, enabling the marshalling of military forces to endangered spots. No, all the evidence points towards our part of the Roman world as being at peace with Rome, or at least cooperative.

Move on a few hundred years and we begin to see the changing face of Britain, forts hurriedly refortified against the ever growing threat from seasonal Saxon raiding parties and later, mobile mounted armies seeking conquest and settlement. It's the period during which Arthurian legends grew and went on to be linked with Alfred in his fight against yet new threats, this time from Scandinavian forces three hundred years or so later. This brings us full circle to the 'herepaths', the term used by the Anglo-Saxon settlers for the green tracks used by the armies. These linked in with the more ancient Ridgeway, giving access to the heartland of ancient Britain and the wealth it held and still does. Whilst cattle may not play such an important role in the economy of the area, cereal production and the rearing of horses still very much does.

16. Streatley and 'The tale of the Frenchman'.

Streatley, along with its larger neighbour Goring, straddle the river Thames. Here was a crossing of the Thames by means of a ford, allowing both man and beast to negotiate the river during favourable conditions. Fording of the river on foot, however, would have been a hazardous undertaking at the best of times. The banks most likely were unmanaged, the gap in the chalk ridge effectively a restricted floodplain. This crossing point of such an important waterway led to the establishment of the twin settlements we see today. A ferry is known to have plied the river since at least the mediaeval period under the auspices of Goring Priory, thereby allowing passage unhindered by the level of the water for the most part. It was not until 1838 that a wooden bridge was constructed, in turn being replaced by the present concrete one in 1920.

With the passage of man and beast came trade and prosperity resulting in the establishment of inns, shops and churches to cater for both the secular and spiritual needs of the traveller. At the time of my first visit to Streatley, around 1971, I was reliably informed that the Swan Inn, a former coaching inn beside the present bridge, was owned by Danny La Rue. As to whether this so called 'reliable' information was correct and just what difference that made, I failed to appreciate then, as I do now! On a later visit we stopped for lunch at another hostelry at the start of a trek to Swindon along The Ridgeway. It was a very hot summers day and the thought of a cold glass of cider accompanied by a good 'ploughman's' in the shade seemed agreeable. Unfortunately it was not to be. Oh the cider was good enough and we did find a shaded spot outside on the terraced patio. It was the so-called 'ploughman's' that left me rattled. It was around the beginning of the 1970's that 'pub-grub' really took off with public houses vying with one another to entice in the now ever growing public seeking the country experience. As a consequence certain establishments went up-market, the menus became extensive and in a lot of cases quite inappropriate. Exotic dishes along with the 'sexing up' of otherwise traditional fare such as the humble 'ploughman's' now became the norm. The consequence was that costs soared and it became increasingly difficult to find a descent plain watering hole that offered simple honest food at reasonable prices.

The traditional 'ploughman's' had consisted of a hunk of crusty bread, a good portion of local hard cheese and raw onion, washed down with copious amounts of rough cider. Obviously when not in the field but the local, then certain refinements crept in, a little pickle, a tomato and butter perhaps. All this could be had for a couple of 'bob' (10p in the coinage of today), the cider being extra. Well now we were being asked to pay around five shillings (25p) for what was in effect a full-blown salad with an assortment of biscuits, cheeses, pickles and bread. This being our last possible place to get any refreshment prior to setting off on our walk, we felt we had no alternative but to go for it. At first glance the meal looked reasonably good, but the cheese was lacking, as was the bread. Over all was a deposit of salad made up mainly of limp lettuce. The latter I left, as I couldn't bring myself to eat the numerous greenfly that clung to the leaves. We left the pub moaning to ourselves, not to the management. Now it would be different, times have changed and it is accepted that to complain is everyone's right, besides, being wiser makes a difference, that and being a grumpy old man!

Meanwhile, back in the early 1970's and at the end of long hot walk from Swindon to Streatley along with three friends, a night was spent camping on the outskirts of the village. I say a long walk as we had camped the previous night at Wayland's Smithy, the intervening distance being some 18 miles. My companions not being used to walking such long distances, Streatley proper proved to be a mile or so too far. We had stopped short, finding a place to pitch our tents in a field near to Warren Cottage beneath Thurle Down. Advice had been sought on where we could camp from the occupant of a cottage alongside the track leading up to the farm. The occupant in this case was an elderly Frenchman. Thus follows what was to become known to our small party of friends as 'The tale of The Frenchman'.

We had arrived at the cottage late in the day, very tired and in need of a place to pitch for the night, to acquire some water and space to prepare a meal. Knocking on the door we were greeted by the tall thin stooping figure of an elderly man. Immediately he spoke it was apparent that he was French, which in those days was something of a novelty to us. Having succinctly explained what it was we required 'The Frenchman' in turn, in his broken English, invited us into the cottage for refreshments. Biscuits and a pot of tea were produced and we sat around the scrubbed wooden table in what was a small bare kitchen that passed as the living room of the house. During the following conversation we learnt a little of the circumstances in which 'The Frenchman' came to be living where he was. He was serving in the French army during the First World War when he had been wounded during an offensive and basically left for dead on the battlefield. However his luck was in as a British officer came across him and realising he was still alive, managed to carry him back to the safety of the allied lines where he was treated for his wounds. The British Officer had saved 'The Frenchman's' life at no little risk to his own. The following part of the story is somewhat blurred, partly due to 'The Frenchman's' pigeon English, but more down to my poor memory! Anyway, following the rescue a friendship was struck up between the 'The Frenchman' and the British officer. The former vowed he would in turn look out for the officer should he ever need his assistance. What transpired is that the British officer was himself to become incapacitated; whether through later illness or injuries sustained on the battlefield I cannot say. However, when 'The Frenchman' heard of this he sought out 'his' officer and acted on the pledge he had made.

At this point 'The Frenchman' took us through to the other downstairs room. Here was an emancipated figure lying in a bed surrounded by books, photographs, clothes and odd bits of furniture. All was a mess and the smell of stale urine filled the air. The officer, for that is who this poor feeble person was, looked confused and remained silent as 'The Frenchman' introduced us and told him about our plight. We stood around the bed feeling a little awkward as it became obvious that here was an old soldier who was slipping towards the last post; his only contact with the outside world and reality, the companion who cared for him to the best of his ability. 'The Frenchman' had kept to his personal pledge and was still 'looking out' for his friend some fifty years on! As we moved back into the kitchen 'The Frenchman' told us we could camp in the paddock behind the cottage, help ourselves to water as the backdoor was always open, as was the outside toilet. Upon leaving to sort ourselves out and prepare a meal 'The Frenchman' invited us to come back for a drink later in the evening.

The tents pitched and a meal eaten, we discussed 'The Frenchman's' offer of a drink. We were divided the two girls were hesitant while us two lads were openly pleased by the offer. The girls seemed to think the old man had ulterior motives and found him and the whole set-up strange and unnerving. We for our part felt that he was just being friendly and that he probably was only too pleased to have a little company for a change. The girls were adamant, no way were they going back into the house. The outcome of all this was that we two lads decided we would take up the invitation, not wishing to hurt the old man's feelings. The girls settled down in their tent after first getting us to leave the camping axe, a torch and sheaf-knife with them! Quite what they thought this old Frenchman of around eighty was capable of, I'm not too sure. Returning to the cottage we were greeted by 'The Frenchman' who asked why the girls were not with us. "Oh they're tired from the days walk and just wanted to sleep" was our honest and at the same time guarded reply. Sitting back down at the kitchen table we produced a hip flask of whisky and an assortment of bits of food as a sort of contribution towards the evening. 'The Frenchman' was obviously appreciative of our gesture and thanked us. There naturally followed a lot of talk and some drinking, the whisky supplemented by coffee, wine and more food. That hour or so flew by before we returned to the tents. The girls however were very much awake and only gave into sleep once we had assured them that there really was nothing to fear from our host.

Looking back on that incident I have often wondered just how 'The Frenchman' had ended up looking after 'his' officer and how it was they had found themselves living in what appeared to be a tied cottage. There are a lot of unanswered questions. Did the two men return to England during the war? Did 'The Frenchman' come to the officer's aid years later? What relationship did they have, friends, officer and batman, lovers? We shall probably never know, but what I do know is that a bond had developed between the two men in the heat of battle, which went further than mere friendship. Here then were two elderly men living in very basic conditions, one confused and vulnerable, the other apparently contented with his lot as carer and companion.

17. The tales end.

With the forty mile stretch of the Ridgeway having now been looked at, discussed and generally put under the eye glass, I shall bring this collection of tales and observations to a close. But as is the case in so many instances of looking into the history of a place, or area and reminiscing, there's always one last story to tell, one last snippet of information and this is no exception.

Briefly then are two final offerings. The first is to draw your attention to what to many walkers on The Ridgeway goes unnoticed, a small stone memorial. By the way, as it's been a long time since I saw this for myself, the exact location is a little hazy in my mind; therefore this should prove a challenge for some of you! The stone in question lies alongside the track on its north side, to the east of the crossing of The Ridgeway at Gore Hill, by the A34, if I'm not mistaken. This little memorial is dedicated to the memory of an army motorcycle despatch rider and marks the spot where he lost his life in an accident whilst on manoeuvres. Here then is a tangible reminder of the folly of war, this poor chap dying before even getting anywhere near the battlefield. It should also act as a warning to those who choose to use The Ridgeway as a location for motorcycle dirt track scrambling. Use this green track in this way then you use it at your peril!

Whilst on the subject of motorcycles, this brings me to my last reminiscence. Back in the early 70's I was want to go walking around Christmas and New Year. On this particular occasion I set out from Swindon on my old Vespa 90 scooter, in falling snow, for Foxhill near to Wanborough. My intention was to walk The Ridgeway to Wayland's Smithy and back, a distance of some eight miles. By the time I reached the inn at Foxhill 'the snow lay all around deep and crisp and even', as the words of the carol goes. My first problem was to release myself from the rubber grips to the handlebars of my scooter, both my leather gauntlets and hands being frozen. This finally accomplished, I prepared myself for the walk. Once off the road the snow was ankle deep and up to my knees and beyond the further I advanced up the track to below the summit of Charlbury Hill. The way ahead looked daunting. Hey but what the heck, I was young and full of vigour, a little snow wasn't going to stop me. My advance was slow to say the least. I crossed the minor road coming up out of Bishopstone that gives access to Bishopstone Downs and trudged on doggedly. The day was bright and no snow now fell but it was bitter cold. Just two more miles and I came to the crossing of the Ashbury to Lambourn road and the realisation that to go further would be lunacy! I was cold, I hadn't seen another living person and the weather was not improving. My objective remained allusive as I retraced my steps arriving back at Foxhill frozen to the core and tired beyond any previous experience. That day had taught me to respect the weather, especially in what many people would see as a tranquil, soft part of the country. Appearances can be very deceptive and in conditions such as those, if my bravado had gotten the better of me, could well have proved fatal. I returned home that day thankful of the mountain training I had received in the Brecon Beacons during outward-bound courses I'd attended.

My recollections began in the area of my town of birth, Swindon and have fanned out to encompass the length of the chalk escarpment running from Streatley and Goring on

Thames south and west to the area around Avebury. In all these tales I have shared with you my own personal views on what I have seen and how I interpret the landscape and the places within it. Obviously I have drawn upon other people's research and writings, but for the best part the observations and conclusions are my own, along with any factual errors and misconceptions!

It's been over forty five years since I first began to explore The Ridgeway under my own steam. During this time I have seen many changes in the landscape, some major, many minor. Along with these changes, I too have changed. My knowledge has grown as I have matured so that my understanding has affected the way in which I interpret these changes. In many ways a lifetime spent in seeking out information may be compared to the linear form of The Ridgeway itself. In its early stage, its birth if you like, it saunters along after leaving the Thames. Then comes the chalk escarpment and with it a sudden rise up onto the hills. This I see as the steep learning curve one goes though in those formative years between the ages of three and six. This is followed by undulating hilly country before the crest of the escarpment is reached proper. Here then are those junior years spent in acquiring the basics, the foundation of our understanding. Next are the clear open views down into The Vale of the White Horse with the main track heading on purposefully into the distance and side branches leading off into the unknown Surely we have here mainstream schooling with its clear objectives and well laid-out plan with university on the horizon as a goal? But as is always the case in life, those branches can lead to dead ends, to fuzzy areas where you're not quite sure as to their relevance. Along the way, all seems straightforward until the odd dip or diversion is encountered as around Chiseldon Plain. Decisions have to be made. Do I keep to the high ground, which involves going those extra few miles? Or do I take the direct route, which involves ups and downs? Life is much the same, to play it safe or to take the odd gamble? Whatever course is taken, the tracks converge and you proceed on your way, the clear open views to one side opening up again, gentle sloping Downs to the other before yet another decision has to be made as to whether to continue directly on to The Sanctuary, or take the tempting track, The Herepath, down into Avebury. Might this not represent being in a steady career and stable relationship with the ever-present temptation of something, or someone, perceived as being better? Invariably that decision is made, with some choosing to continue direct to the obvious termination of the route whilst others take in the detour and some would say the best of both worlds! But what lies beyond? I hear you ask. Well I for one don't know, but if it's anything like the countryside beyond The Sanctuary, then it'll be fragmented.

The above may seem to be pure fantasy, trivial nonsense and I would to the greater part agree. But for many who go in search of the meaning of life, our distant ancestors along with the remains of their cultures provide a crutch on which to hang half-baked beliefs, fanciful ideas, or perhaps more realistically, to lean! You only have to stop and look around such places as Glastonbury, Stonehenge and, my own personally much loved, Avebury to see how some in society have hijacked and belittled these truly atmospheric locations. I would ask you the reader to take another look, a deeper look, then like me you may be filled not with the so called magic of the area, but the more meaningful feeling of place, of belonging, of heritage.

The Ridgeway then can be seen as a metaphor for life, and still is I'm sure, by many. Walk the green track and you tread in the footsteps of your forebears, our ancestors.

Clive R. Bowd.   February 2017.

Bibliography.

The following books and booklets have been consulted and are in all probability now out of print. But if you can run down a copy of 'The Oldest Road', you would be hard pressed to find a better introduction to this fascinating part of our heritage.

Anderson & Godwin. (1975). The Oldest Road. An Exploration of The Ridgeway. Wildwood House. London.

Crompton P. (1969). The Prehistoric Ridge Way. A Journey. Abingdon.

Disbury D. (1974). On and Around White Horse Hill. Disbury. Egham.

Pearson J. (1979). Richard Jefferies. Landscape & Labour. Moonraker Press. Bradford-on-Avon.

Pocock E. (1964). The Mystery of White Horse Hill. Pocock. Clanfield, Oxon.

Street P. (1971). Portrait of Wiltshire. Robert Hale & Co. London.

Printed in Great Britain
by Amazon

55370434R00038